Portraits in Plaster, Collection of Lauren

Laurence Hutton

Alpha Editions

This edition published in 2024

ISBN 9789361470752

Design and Setting By

Alpha Editions

www.alphaedis.com

Email - info@alphaedis.com

Contents

INTRODUCTION.

The story of the beginning of my collection of masks is curious and perhaps interesting. The half-dozen casts upon which it is based were found, early in the Sixties, in a dust-bin in one of the old-fashioned streets which run towards the East River, in the neighborhood of Tompkins Square, New York. Their owner had lately died; his unsympathetic and unappreciative heirs had thrown away what they considered "the horrible things;" a small boy had found them, and offered them for sale to a dealer in phrenological casts, who realized their worth, although, in many cases, he did not know whose heads they represented; and so, by chance, they came into my possession, and inspired the search for more.

The history of these masks which formed the nucleus of the collection, or the history of the original collector himself, I have never been able to discover. They are, however, the casts most frequently described in the printed lectures of George Combe, who came to America in the winter of 1838-39, and the inference is that they were left here by him in the hands of one of his disciples.

The earliest masks in the collection to-day are replicas of those of Dante, made, perhaps, in the first part of the fourteenth century, and of Tasso, certainly made at the end of the sixteenth. The latest mask is that of Edwin Booth, who died only a few months ago. They range from Sir Isaac Newton, the wisest of men, to Sambo, the lowest type of the American negro; from Oliver Cromwell to Henry Clay; from Bonaparte to Grant; from Keats to Leopardi; from Pius IX. to Thomas Paine; from Ben Caunt, the prize-fighter, to Thomas Chalmers, the light of the Scottish pulpit.

So far as I have been able to discover, mine is the most nearly complete and the largest collection of its kind in the world. I have, indeed, found nothing anywhere to compare with it. Usually, the Phrenological Museums contain casts of idiots, criminals, and monstrosities, and these are seemingly gathered together to illustrate what man's cranial structure ought not to be. There are but three or four casts of the faces of distinguished persons in the British Museum, and about as many in the National Portrait Gallery in London; and all of these I am able to present here, with the exception of that of James II., who belongs, perhaps, to the criminal class. In the Hohenzollern Museum are many casts, but these generally are those of civic or national celebrities—Berlin aldermen or German warriors, in whom the world at large has but little interest. The casts of Frederick the Great, Queen Louise, Schiller, and one or two more in that institution, however, I was permitted to have reproduced. The others I have gathered after many years of patient and pleasant research in the studios, the curiosity-shops, and the plaster-shops of most of the capitals of Europe and America. The story of this research, with an account of the means taken to identify the masks when they were discovered, could itself make a book of this size. I am sure that mine is the actual death-mask of Aaron Burr, for instance, because I have the personal guarantee of the man who made the mould in 1836; I am positive of the identity of another cast, because I saw it made myself; and concerning still another, I have no question, because I know the man who stole it! In the matter of the great majority of the masks, however, the difficulties were very great. Hardly one *per centum* of the hundreds of biographers whose works I have consulted ever refer to the taking of a mask in life, or after death, and there is absolutely no literature which is devoted to the subject. The cast of Sheridan's hand is often alluded to, the mask of his dead face is nowhere mentioned; and yet there appears to be no doubt that both were taken. The cast of his head has been compared carefully with all the existing portraits; it has been examined by experts in portraiture; phrenologists have described the character of the man most accurately, from its bumps and its physiognomy; it was certainly made from nature; it is too like Sheridan to have been made from the nature of any other man; and yet there is no record of its having been made. No surviving member of the family of Coleridge had ever heard of the existence of his death-mask until my copy was discovered, but they all accept it as genuine; and I recognized Mr. Ernest Hartley Coleridge once, in the corridor of a London club, by his wonderful resemblance in features, and in the shape of his head, to the mask of his grandfather. The mask of Dean Swift which I possess is exactly like the long-lost cast as it is engraved in Dr. Wilde's book. The mask of Charles XII. shows distinctly the marks of the bullet in the temple; and I have succeeded in tracing the other casts in many and very different ways.

I may mention here that some of these masks, as you now see them, were broken in the Custom-house in New York, and that the mask of Elihu Burritt was demolished entirely and without hope of restoration. Upon these, notwithstanding their condition, and upon all the imported masks, I paid a duty of fifty-five *per centum*, upon a valuation assessed usually at twenty-five *per centum* above what I swore was their value in Europe; the Custom-house charges of various kinds being, in many instances, larger than the original cost of the casts themselves. So far as I can understand, I was taxed in this matter in order to protect the ghosts of the plasterers of America, who could not have made these casts even if they had so wished!

The value of a plaster cast as a portrait of the dead or living face cannot for a moment be questioned. It must, of necessity, be absolutely true to nature.

It cannot flatter; it cannot caricature. It shows the subject as he was, not only as others saw him, in the actual flesh, but as he saw himself. And in the case of the death-mask particularly, it shows the subject often as he permitted no one but himself to see himself. He does not pose; he does not "try to look pleasant." In his mask he is seen, as it were, with his mask off!

Lavater, in his *Physiognomy*, says that "the dead, and the impressions of the dead, taken in plaster, are not less worthy of observation [than the living faces]. The settled features are much more prominent than in the living and in the sleeping. What life makes fugitive, death arrests. What was undefinable is defined. All is reduced to its proper level; each trait is in its true proportion, unless excruciating disease or accident have preceded death." And Mr. W. W. Story, in writing of the life-mask of Washington, says of life-masks generally: "Indeed a mask from the living face, though it repeats exactly the true forms of the original, lacks the spirit and expression of the real person. But this is not always the case. The more mobile and variable the face, the more the mask loses; the more set and determined the character and expression, the more perfectly the work reproduces it."

The procedure of taking a mould of the living face is not pleasant to the subject. In order to prevent the adhesion of the plaster, a strong lather of soap and water, or more frequently a small quantity of oil, is applied to the hair and to the beard. This will explain the flat and unnatural appearance of the familiar mustache and imperial in the cast of Napoleon III. In some instances, as in that of Keats, a napkin is placed over the hair. The face is then moistened with sweet-oil; quills are inserted into the nostrils in order that the victim may breathe during the operation, or else openings are left in the plaster for that purpose. A description of the taking of the mould of the face of a Mr. A—— (condensed from a copy of the *Phrenological Journal*, published in Edinburgh in January, 1845), will give the uninitiated some idea of the process: "The person was made to recline on his back at an angle of about thirty-five degrees, and upon a seat ingeniously adapted to the purpose. The hair and the face being anointed with a little pure scented oil, the plaster was laid carefully upon the nose, mouth, eyes, and forehead, in such a way as to avoid disturbing the features; and this being set, the back of the head was pressed into a flat dish containing plaster, where it continued to recline, as on a pillow. The plaster was then applied to the parts of the head still uncovered, and soon afterwards the mould was hard enough to be removed in three pieces, one of which, covering the occiput, was bounded anteriorly by a vertical section immediately behind the ears, and the other two, which covered the rest of the head, were divided from each other by pulling up a strong silken thread previously so disposed upon the face on one side of the nose." The account closes with the statement that "Mr. A—— declared that he had been as comfortable as possible all the time"!

Since these papers originally appeared in HARPER'S MAGAZINE in the autumn of 1892, they have been revised, enlarged, and virtually rewritten. Eighteen new masks are here presented, and I have added many pages to the descriptive text.

The subject-matter of the volume may not be considered very cheerful reading, but I feel that to those to whom the work appeals at all it will appeal strongly as an unique portrait gallery of men and women of all countries and of many ages, distinguished in many walks of life. I trust that it will lend itself particularly to extra-illustration. And to all those who make human portraiture a study, or a hobby, it is cordially inscribed.

LAURENCE HUTTON.

NEW YORK, January 1, 1894.

PORTRAITS IN PLASTER

"The sleeping and the dead are but as pictures."

—*Macbeth*, act ii., scene 2.

If the creator of Duncan was right in saying that there is no art to find the mind's construction in the face, then must the author of the *Novum Organum* have been wrong when he declared that "physiognomy ... discovereth the disposition of the mind by the lineaments of the body;" and these, curiously enough, are parallel passages never quoted by the believers in the theory that Bacon was the writer of Shakspere's plays.

It is not intended here to enter into a discussion of the merits or demerits of physiognomy. This is an Exhibition of Portraits, not a Phrenological Lecture. I shall try to show how these men and women looked, in life and in death, not why they happened to look as they did; and I shall dwell generally upon their brains, occasionally upon their bones, but only incidentally upon their bumps.

The ancient Romans are said to have made, in wax, casts of the faces of their illustrious dead. These masks are believed to have been colored to represent the originals as they appeared in life, to have been cherished religiously by their descendants through many generations, and, on the occasion of a public and formal funeral, it is thought that they were sometimes worn by professional mourners, as a sort of posthumous tribute from the dead already to the memory of the latest man who had died. And recent explorers have satisfied themselves that in the early burials of many nations it was the custom to cover the heads and bodies of the dead with sheets of gold so pliable that they took the impress of the form; and not infrequently, when in the course of centuries the embalmed flesh had shrivelled or fallen away, the gold retained the exact cast of the features. Schliemann found a number of bodies "covered with large masks of gold-plate in *repoussé*-work," several of which have been reproduced by means of engraving, in his *Mycenæ*; and he asserted that there can be no doubt whatever that each one of these represents the likeness of the deceased person whose face it covered.

When Hamlet said that Alexander died, Alexander was buried, Alexander returneth to dust, he overlooked the fact that Alexander's dust, instead of being converted into loam to stop a beer-barrel, was preserved from corruption by the process of embalming, and from external injury by being cased in the most precious of metals. Pettigrew, in his *History of Egyptian Mummies*, said of the death-mask of Alexander that "it was a sort of chase-work, and of such a nature that it could be applied so closely to the skin as to preserve not only the form of the body, but also to give the expression of the features to the countenance." He did not quote his authority for this statement, but it is unquestionably derived from the account of the death and burial of Alexander written by Diodorus Siculus, who said: "And first a coffin of beaten gold was provided, so wrought by the hammer as to answer to the proportions of the body; it was half filled with aromatic spices, which served as well to delight the sense as to prevent the body from putrefaction." Then follows a description of the funeral chariot, and of the long line of march from Babylon to Alexandria, where Augustus Cæsar saw the tomb three hundred years later; but there is no reference to a mask of Alexander's face in gold. It is greatly to be regretted that such a mask does not exist now, that it might be compared with the plaster masks of Cromwell, Washington, Frederick the Great, Bonaparte, Grant, and Sherman, and other conquerors of later days here presented to the public scrutiny.

Among the gold mummy-masks exhibited in the Museum of the Louvre is one, as Mr. John C. Van Dyke points out, which bears a curious and striking resemblance not only to Washington, but to the familiar portraits of Greuze, the painter. It is No. 536 of the Egyptian Collection, and bears a card with the following inscription: "Masque de Momie trouvé dans le chambre d'Apis consacré par le Prince Kha-Em-Onas."

In the collection of antiques presented to the museum at Naples by Prince Corignano is a wax mask with glass eyes. It was found with four decapitated bodies in a tomb at Cumæ, and it is evidently a portrait of the original, who is said to have been a Christian martyr. And Mr. W. M. Flynders Petrie exhibited in London, in the autumn of 1892, an exceedingly interesting collection of antiquities brought from Tel-el-Amarna, the Arab name for the ancient city of Khuenaten, situated about one hundred and eighty miles south of Cairo. That city was built about fourteen hundred years before Christ, by Khuenaten, son of Amenhotep III., who made it the centre of his proposed great revolution in religion, art, and ethics. The collection comprised, among other things, a cast from the head of Khuenaten himself, taken after death, according to Mr. Petrie, for the use of the sculptor who was preparing the sarcophagus for his tomb. These are among the earliest examples of death-masks which have come down to us.

At least three copies of the Dante mask, all believed to be authentic, are known to be in existence. First, that which is called the Torrigiani cast, which can be traced back to 1750; second, the so-called Seymour Kirkup mask, given to him by the sculptor Bartolini, who is said to have found it in Ravenna; and third, a mask belonging, according to Kirkup, to "the late sculptor Professor Ricci." "The slight differences between these," adds Kirkup, "are such as might occur in casts made from the original mask." Concerning the original mask itself, says Mr. Charles Eliot Norton, there is no trustworthy history to be obtained. On the very threshold of his inquiry into the matter he was met with the doubt whether the art of taking casts was practised at the time of Dante's death at all, Vasari, in his life of Andrea del Verocchio, who flourished in the middle of the fifteenth century, having declared that the art first came into use in Verocchio's day. It is certain that there is no record of the Dante mask for three hundred years after Dante died; but it is equally certain that it resembles nearly all the portraits of Dante down to the time of Raphael. Mr. Norton believes, from external evidence, that it is, at all events, a death-mask of some one; and of this, it seems to me, there can be no question.

There are two masks of Dante now on public exhibition in Florence. One is in the house built upon the site of the mansion in which Dante was born; the other is in a small cabinet adjoining the Hall of the Hermaphrodite in the Uffizi Gallery. The former is a cast of the face only, and it bears every evidence of recent construction. The latter is a cast in plaster of the head and shoulders, and is one of the masks of which Mr. Norton speaks. It has, unfortunately, been painted, the face a flesh color, the cap and gown red, the waistcoat and the tabs over the ears green; but it is undoubtedly a very early cast from the mould made from the actual head. It bears the following inscription, "Effigie di Dante Alighieri, Maschera Formata sul di lui Cadavere in Ravenna l'Anno 1321," and to it is attached a card saying that it was bequeathed to the Museum by the Marquis Torrigiani in 1865. It is here reproduced.

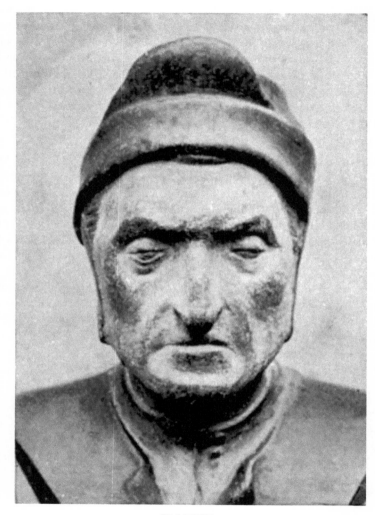

DANTE

"Why keep you your eyes closed, Signor Torquato?" said a watcher at the death-bed of Tasso—one of those silly persons who ask silly questions, even under the most serious circumstances—"Why keep you your eyes closed?" "That they may grow accustomed to remain closed," was the feeble reply. They have been closed to all mortal vision for three hundred years now, but in the pale, cold plaster of the accompanying mask his face is still seen as it was seen by the vast and sorrowing multitudes who lined the streets of Rome to look upon his triumphant funeral procession. His body was clad in an antique toga, kindled tapers lighted his way, and his pallid brow was at last encircled by the wreath of laurel he had waited for so long. And thus at the end of the Nineteenth Century do we, in the New World, look upon the cast of the actual face of the great poet of the Old World who died at the end of the century he adorned. The original mask is preserved, with other personal relics of Tasso, in the room of the convent of San Onofrio, in which he died. But the great powder explosion which shook all Rome a few years ago so shattered this part of the convent that the room and the mask are no longer shown to the public.

The personal appearance of Tasso has been carefully and minutely described by his friend and biographer Manso. His broad forehead was high and inclined to baldness; his thin hair was of a lighter color than that of his countrymen generally; his eyes were large, dark blue, and set wide apart; his eyebrows were black and arched; his nose was aquiline; his mouth was wide; his lips were thin; and his beard was thick and of a reddish-brown tinge.

Tasso went from Naples to Rome to receive from the hands of the Pope the crown of bay which had been worn by Petrarch and other laureates of Italy; and he died upon the day set apart for his coronation.

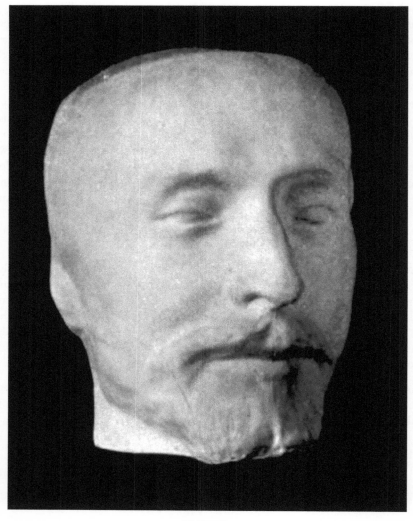

TASSO

The head of Shakspere here presented, from the monumental bust in the chancel of the church at Stratford, like everything else relating to Shakspere, in life or in death, is shrouded in mystery. It is supposed to be the work of one Gerard Johnson, and to have been "cut from a death-mask" shortly after Shakspere's funeral. The earliest allusion to it is to be found in a poem of Leonard Digges, written seven years later. It was certainly in existence during the lifetime of Anne Hathaway Shakspere, and of other members of his family, who would, perhaps, have objected or protested if the likeness had not been considered a good one. Sir Francis Chantrey believed it to have been worked from a cast of the living or the dead face. "There are in the original in the church," he wrote, "marks of individuality which are not to be observed in the usual casts from it; for instance, the markings about the eyes, the wrinkles on the forehead, and the undercutting from the moustachios." Wordsworth, among others, accepted its authenticity, and Mr. Halliwell-Phillipps did not hesitate to put himself on record, more than once, as having every faith in its superiority, in the matter of actual resemblance, to any of the alleged portraits. He ranked it, in point of authority, before the Droeshout print, endorsed by Ben Jonson as perfect; and he called attention to the general resemblance to be traced between them.

It certainly differs in many respects from the famous plaster cast found in a curiosity-shop in Germany some years ago, and known as the Kesselstadt mask, a photograph of which is here reproduced. This mask is believed, by those who believe in it at all, to have been made from Shakspere's dead face, to have been carried to Germany by a German envoy to England in the reign of James I., to have been cherished as an authentic and valuable relic for many generations, to have been sold for rubbish at the death of the last of the race, and to have been recovered in a most fortuitous way. It bears upon its back the date of Shakspere's death, 1616, it has been the subject of more discussion than any piece of plaster of its size in the world, and even those who believe that it is not Shakspere have never asserted that it *is* Bacon!

According to Mr. G. Huntley Gordon, this cast from the Stratford bust was taken about 1845, stealthily and in the middle of the night, by a young Stratford plasterer, who was frightened by imaginary noises before he succeeded in getting a mould of the entire head. After the protest raised against Malone for whitewashing the bust in 1793, the authorities, naturally, had put an embargo upon any handling of the monument, and the operation was fraught with much risk to the aspiring youth who undertook it. A cast is known to have been taken for Malone, however, and since then other casts have been made by other artists, notably one by George Bullock, who made the death-mask of Scott.

SHAKSPERE—Stratford Bust

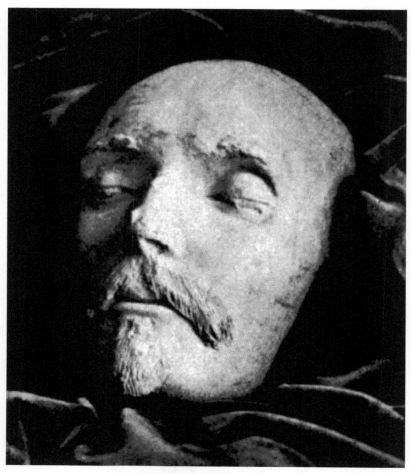

SHAKSPERE—Kesselstadt Mask

Next to the Stratford bust, the sculptured portrait of Shakspere most familiar to the world is that which stands in Poets' Corner, Westminster Abbey. The artist went to some strange source for the likeness, and although it was for gentle Shakspere cut, by no means does it outdo the life. "I saw old Samuel Johnson," said Cumberland, describing Garrick's funeral—"I saw old Samuel Johnson standing at the foot of Shakspere's monument, and bathed in tears." Burke on that occasion remarked that the statue of Shakspere looked towards Garrick's grave; and on this stray hint, as Mr. Brander Matthews believes, Sheridan hung his famous couplet in the *Monody*:

"While Shakspere's image, from its hallowed base,

Served to prescribe the grave and point the place."

Garrick's face, it is said, was wonderfully under control, and his features had a marvellous flexibility, which rendered variety and rapid change of expression an easy matter. The story of his having frightened Hogarth by standing before him as the ghost of Fielding, assuming the appearance of the dead novelist in all the fixedness and rigidity of death, has often been told. There are many original portraits of Garrick in existence. The Garrick Club in London possesses at least a dozen, while The Players in New York own two by Zoffany, and one by Reynolds.

A not uncommon print, entitled "The Mask of Garrick taken from the Face after Death," is in the Shaksperian Library at Stratford-upon-Avon, and it is to be found in Evans's "Catalogue of Engraved Portraits." It does not seem, however, to be the portrait of a dead man, being full of living expression, and it is, perhaps, an enlarged reproduction of the face in the miniature by Pine of Bath, now in the Garrick Club, the eyes having the same dilatation of pupil which was characteristic of the great actor.

The mask here shown was purchased in 1876 from the late Mr. Marshall, the antiquarian dealer in Stratford, who possessed what he believed to be its pedigree written in pencil on the back of the plaster, and now unfortunately defaced. He asserted that it was taken from life, and that it had come by direct descent from the sculptor's hands into his. There is a replica of it in the Shakspere Museum at Stratford, but no history is attached to it, and the trustees know nothing about it, except that it was "the gift of the late Miss Wheeler." It resembles very strongly the familiar portrait of Garrick by Hogarth, the original of which hangs in one of the bedrooms of Windsor Castle.

DAVID GARRICK

In a very early cast of the Garrick mask, still existing in London, the texture of the skin proves conclusively that it was taken from nature, and most probably from life.

In the "Guild Hall" of "The City of Lushington," an ancient and very unique social club, which has met for many years in a dark and dingy little back room connected with the Harp Tavern, in Russell Street, Covent Garden, London, are still preserved the chair of Edmund Kean, the hole in the wall made by the quart pot he threw once, in a fit of gross insubordination, at a former "Lord Mayor," and what is religiously considered by all the citizens of Lushington to be a death-mask of Kean himself. This cast is covered with glass and with dust and its history is lost in the mists of time. There is no record of it in the metropolitan archives, the corporation will not permit it to be reproduced, even by photography, and it bears but little resemblance to Kean, or to the mask in my possession, which also has no history, but which I believe to be authentic, and which is certainly very like the sketch of Kean done in oils by George Clint, and now in the possession of Mr. Henry Irving. This hurried sketch of Clint's is said to be the only portrait for which Kean could be induced to sit. It was made in Kean's bedroom in a few hours, and it is the groundwork of more than one finished portrait of the same subject by the same artist. The portrait of Kean by Neagle, now the property of The Players, has a similar tradition.

The Lushington cast is perhaps an early life-mask of the elder Kean, perhaps a life-mask, or a death-mask, of the younger Kean, more probably the mask of some defunct and commonplace and now forgotten mayor or alderman of Lushington, who did not even look like Kean.

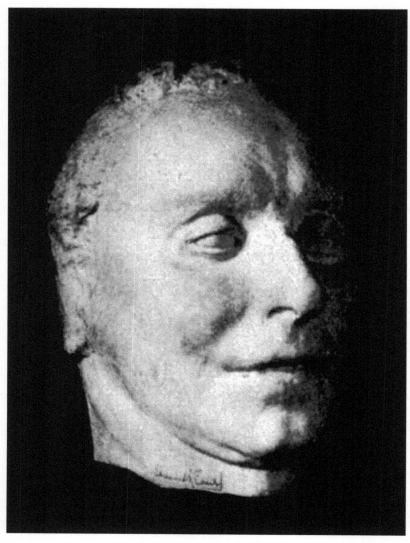

EDMUND KEAN

The eye-witnesses of Kean's theatrical performances were generally so much impressed by the force of his acting that they paid little attention to his personal appearance. We read in Leslie's *Autobiography* that "he had an amazing power of expression in his face," and "that his face, although not handsome, was picturesque;" a writer in the *New Monthly Magazine* in 1833 spoke of him as "a small man with an Italian face and fatal eye;" a writer in *Blackwood*, a few years later, called him "a man of low and meagre figure, of a Jewish physiognomy, and a stifled and husky voice;" while Miss Fanny Kemble said that "he possessed particular physical qualifications; an eye like an orb of light; a voice exquisitely touching and melodious in its tendencies, but in the harsh dissonance of vehement passion terribly true." Barry Cornwall, in his poor *Life of Kean*, spoke of "his thin, dark face, full of meaning, taking, at every turn, a sinister or vigilant expression," and as being "just adapted to the ascetic and revengeful Shylock." And Henry Crabb Robinson said in 1814, "Kean's face is finely expressive, though his mouth is not handsome, and he projects his lower lip ungracefully."

The portrait of Kean by Helen Faucit, Lady Martin, is the best that has been presented to us. She met him once on the Green at Richmond when she was a child, and he a broken-down old man. "I was startled, frightened at what I saw," she wrote: "a small pale man with a fur cap, and wrapped in a fur cloak. He looked to me as if come from the grave. A stray lock of very dark hair crossed his forehead, under which shone eyes which looked dark, and yet bright as lamps. So large were they, so piercing, so absorbing, I could see no other features.... Oh, what a voice was that which spoke! It seemed to come from far away—a long, long way behind him. After the first salutation, it said, 'Who is this little one?' When my sister had explained, the face smiled; I was reassured by the smile, and the face looked less terrible."

Among the English-speaking actors of later days few have been better known and better liked, in America at all events, than John McCullough, Dion Boucicault, Lawrence Barrett, Henry Edwards, and Edwin Booth, the faces of all of whom I am able to present here. John McCullough, the first of this galaxy of stars to quit the stage of life, was a man of strong and attractive personality, if not a great actor; he had many admirers in his profession and many friends out of it. The cloak which Forrest dropped fell upon his shoulders, and in such parts as Virginius, Damon, and the Brutus of John Howard Payne, it was nobly worn. He was as modest, as simple, and as manly in character as are the characters he represented on the stage. Unhappily, mental disease preceded McCullough's death, and during the last few years of his life those who loved him best prayed for the rest which is here shown on his face. The *post-mortem* examination revealed a brain of unusual size and of very high development. The death-mask was made by Mr. H. H. Kitson, of Boston.

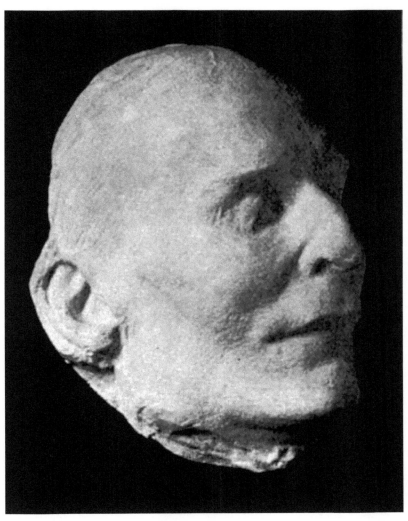

JOHN M'CULLOUGH

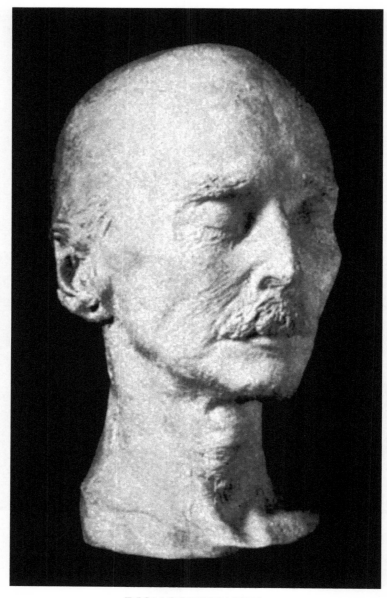

DION BOUCICAULT

Dion Boucicault, worn by age, died in the city of New York in the early autumn of 1890. He was one of the most remarkably versatile men of the century. He was a fairly good actor, an excellent stage-manager, an ingenious stage-machinist, an admirable judge of plays and of the capacities of the men about him, the most entertaining of companions, a man of quick wit, of restless personality, and the author and adapter, perhaps, of more dramatic productions, good and bad, than any man who ever lived. The cast of the head of Boucicault was made the day after his death, by Mr. J. Scott Hartley, of New York.

Of the masks of Lawrence Barrett and of Henry Edwards I can hardly trust myself to speak here or yet. My personal friendship with them was so intimate, my affection so strong, and their taking away so recent, that I can only look upon the casts of their dead faces as I looked upon the dead faces themselves a few months ago, and grieve afresh for what I have lost.

Mr. William Winter, who knew Barrett long and well, has spoken of "his stately head silvered during the last few years with graying hair, of his dark eyes deeply sunken and glowing with intense light, of his thin visage paled with study and with pain, of his form of grace, and of his voice of sonorous eloquence and solemn music, one of the few great voices of this present dramatic generation in its compass, variety, and sweetness. His head was a grand head; his face beautiful in its spirit, its bravery, and its strength." As the Rev. John A. Chadwick finely said of him in the *Christian Register*, "The noblest part he ever acted was the part of Lawrence Barrett—an honest, brave, and kindly gentleman."

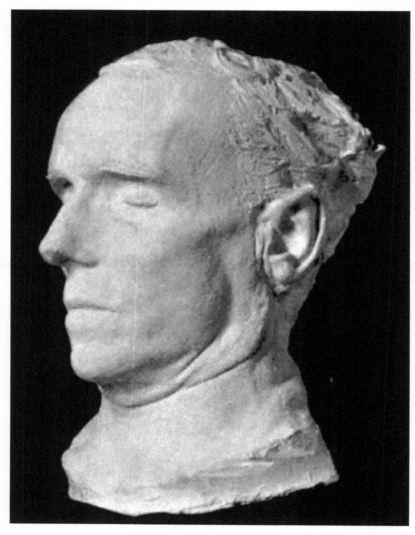

LAWRENCE BARRETT

Mr. Barrett was one of the little party who were with Mr. Booth when the idea of The Players was first conceived, and who helped their friend, the Founder, to bring that association to its present perfected state. Mr. Barrett was one of its legal incorporators; from the beginning until his death he was a member of its governing body, and he was always enthusiastic in his devotion to it, and to the objects for which Mr. Booth had endowed it. At the annual celebration of the club, held upon what is called "Founder's Night," December 31, 1890, Mr. Barrett read aloud, and with a great deal of feeling, in the club-house, Mr. Thomas Bailey Aldrich's touching poem upon Mr. John S. Sargent's portrait of Mr. Booth, and it was noticed by many present that his voice faltered when he spoke of

"Others standing in the place

Where save as ghosts we come no more."

He was himself the first of those present to go to the Land of Shadows. That his gentle spirit haunts the place, and will haunt it pleasantly for many years to come, not one who knew and loved him there can for a moment doubt.

Henry Edwards was not only an actor but a man of science. He was recognized as a distinguished entomologist by many persons on both sides of the Atlantic who had never even heard of his theatrical career. He left a magnificent collection of butterflies, now preserved in one of the leading museums of America, and he contributed to the press of both countries a number of valuable books and pamphlets upon the subject he loved. His work upon the stage was uniformly good. As Mr. Winter said of him, in a funeral oration, he did not astonish and dazzle; he satisfied. He excelled in the representation of rough pathos, of bluff good-humor, and of honest indignation. He had a frank, expressive, cheerful face and a hearty voice. He was a man of genuine, healthy honesty and simplicity, who left behind him many warmly attached friends. He was sympathetic and always interested in anything that interested the men about him. Many a time has he studied, discussed, and moralized over, the collection which now, alas! contains the cast of his own dead face. The mask was made by Mr. J. Scott Hartley.

A death-mask of Booth was taken under the direction of Mr. Augustus St. Gaudens. Although there is about it nothing which is distressing or unpleasant, his family and his friends prefer to have it withheld from the public gaze. The life-mask which, by the courtesy of The Players, prefaces this volume, was made by Mr. John Rogers in 1864, when Booth was in the thirtieth year of his age, and in the zenith of his strength and his beauty.

HENRY EDWARDS

Mrs. Asia Booth Clarke wrote of her brother in 1857: "He had come back [from California] older in experience only, for he looked a boy still, and very fragile; his wild black eyes and long locks gave him an air of melancholy. He had the gentle dignity and inherent grace that one attributes to a young prince; yet he was merry, cheerful, and boyish in disposition, as one can imagine Hamlet to have been in the days before the tragedy was enacted in the orchard."

Mr. Barrett, who supported him in New York a few months later, said: "A slight, pale youth, with black, flowing hair, soft brown eyes, full of tenderness and gentle timidity, a manner mixed with shyness and quiet repose, he took his place [at the first rehearsal] with no air of conquest or self-assertion, and gave his directions with a grace and courtesy which never left him."

Mr. Irving, recalling his earliest associations with Booth in Manchester, in 1861, has told me that the young actor seemed to him at that time to be the most magnificent specimen of intellectual manhood he had ever seen. And George William Curtis, writing in 1864, said: "Booth is altogether princely. His costume is still the solemn suit of sables, varied according to his fancy of greater fitness; and his small, lithe form, with the mobility and intellectual sadness of his face, and his large, melancholy eyes, satisfy the most fastidious imagination that this is Hamlet as he lived in Shakspere's time."

Mrs. M. E. W. Sherwood, speaking of him when he was in his perfect prime, in the part of Othello alludes to "that dark face to which the Eastern robe was so becoming, seeming at once to be telling its mighty story of adventure and conquest. It was a proud and beautiful face. Desdemona was not worthy of it."

Booth's face was to me one of the most beautiful and most lovable that I ever looked upon.

The only feminine heads in the collection graced once the shoulders of a trio of queens, a Queen of Tragedy, a Queen of Prussia, and a Queen of Song. The mask of Mrs. Siddons is in the possession of Mr. Percy Fitzgerald. It is generally accepted as having been taken from the actual face of the great actress, but its pedigree or its history Mr. Fitzgerald does not know.

A bust of Mrs. Siddons by J. Smith, 57 Upper Norton Street, Marylebone, was exhibited in the Model Room of the Royal Academy in 1813, the year before she retired from the stage. Mr. Edward W. Hennell has an autograph letter of Mrs. Siddons, undated and addressed simply "Sir," but written, evidently, to this artist and referring to this bust. In it she says, "The time is drawing near which will bring my labors to an end, and I shall then hope to be able to indulge myself in many gratifications of which they have hitherto deprived me, and among which that of visiting your study will stand very forward."

EDWIN BOOTH

It is not improbable that Smith made a cast of Mrs. Siddons's face, a common occurrence in those days, although unfortunately no such occurrence is recorded by Mrs. Siddons herself, or by any of her biographers.

The present cast is believed by experts to have been taken from life, and at about the time of her retirement. It shows, in a marked degree, the peculiar thickness of the underlip remembered by persons still living who remember Mrs. Siddons, and noticeable in the portraits of all the Kembles of her generation, particularly in those of the great actress herself. The cast resembles strongly an unfinished sketch of her in the South Kensington Museum, made in her old age by an unknown artist, and it is not unlike the bust she made of herself, now in the Dyce Library in the same institution. Other features of Mrs. Siddons were as prominent as her under-lip; Gainsborough is said to have remarked to her once, in a fit of almost inspired courage, "Damn your nose, madam, there is no end to it!" and she herself is reported to have said that "the jaw-bone of the Kembles is as notorious as the jaw-bone used by Samson."

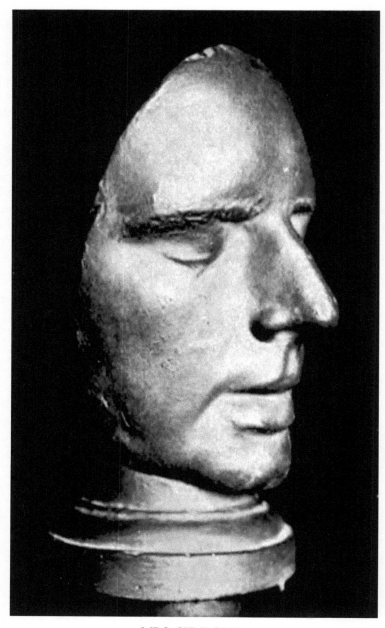

MRS. SIDDONS

The personal appearance of Mrs. Siddons has many times been described, but, curiously enough, none of her contemporaries allude to this unusual development of the lower lip. Mr. Fitzgerald says of her first appearance: "The audience saw a frail, delicate-looking, but pretty creature, tottering towards them rather than walking.... The criticism of the pit amounted to this, 'that she was a pretty, awkward, and interesting creature—frightfully dressed.'" The London *Morning Post*, speaking of the event, said: "Her figure is a very fine one; her features are beautifully expressive; her action is graceful and easy, and her whole deportment that of a gentlewoman." Thomas Davies wrote later: "Just rising above the middle stature, she looks, walks, and moves like a woman of superior rank. Her countenance is expressive, her eye so full of information that the passion is told from her look before she speaks." Madame d'Arblay, in her *Diary* (December 15, 1782), wrote that "she behaved with great propriety; very calm, modest, quiet and unaffected. She has a very fine countenance, and her eyes look both intelligent and soft." Leigh Hunt said, "I did not see her, I believe, in her best days; but she must always have been a somewhat masculine beauty." Peter Irving wrote to his brother Washington in 1813: "I was surprised to find her face, even at the near approach of sitting by her side, absolutely handsome, and unmarked by any of those wrinkles which generally attend advanced life. Her form is at present becoming unwieldy, but not shapeless, and is full of dignity. Her gestures and movements are eminently graceful." Two years later George Ticknor wrote: "She is now, I suppose, sixty years old, and has one of the finest and most spirited countenances and one of the most dignified and commanding persons I ever beheld. Her portraits are very faithful as to her general air and outline, but no art can express or imitate the dignity of her manner, or the intelligent illumination of her face." And John Howard Payne said of her about the same period, 1817: "The grace of her person, the beauty of her arms, the mental beauty of her face, the tragic expression of her voice, and the perfect identification with the character [Mrs. Beverley] left nothing for me to wish for. In these she was so great that even her unwieldy figure, which at first somewhat annoyed me, was soon forgotten."

In 1783 Mrs. Siddons called on Dr. Johnson at Bolt Court, and he gave to Mrs. Thrale an account of how she impressed him by her "modesty and propriety." He says they "talked of plays," but, unfortunately, he does not permit himself to say what he thought of her nose or her mouth or her jaw.

The beautiful Louise of Prussia, mother of the first Emperor William of Germany, lies in the family mausoleum at Charlottenburg, and the cast of her dead face, with that of Frederick the Great and of others of their distinguished countrymen and countrywomen, is preserved in the Museum of Berlin. Her last illness was severe and painful, but her attendants have left on record the fact that in her rare intervals of relief from suffering "she was very tranquil, and lay looking like an angel;" that "the countenance was beautiful in death, particularly the brow; and that the calm expression of the mouth told that the struggle was forever past."

At the age of sixteen she was thus described: "She was like her sister Charlotte—had the same loving blue eyes, but the expression changed more quickly with the feeling or thought of the moment. Her soft brown hair still retained a gleam of the golden tints of childhood; her fair, transparent complexion was, in the bloom of its exquisite beauty, painted by nature as softly as were the roses she gathered and enjoyed. The princess was tall and slight, and graceful in her movements. This grace was not merely external; it arose from the inner depths of a pure and noble mind, and therefore was so full of soul."

LOUISE OF PRUSSIA

Madame Malibran, the Queen of Song, died in Manchester, England, in 1836. The mask here reproduced came, perhaps, from the collection of George Combe, who visited America a few years later.

In *The Memoirs of Malibran*, by the Countess de Merlin, is the emphatic statement that out of respect to the wishes of M. de Beriot, the husband of Malibran, no posthumous sketch or cast of her face of any kind was taken. M. Edmond Cottinet, however, in a private note to Mrs. Clara Bell, wrote: "When Madame Malibran died I was very young, but I remember distinctly hearing my mother told that de Beriot, the husband of her friend, had taken her mask, and that it had helped him to execute the crowned bust of the great singer which now decorates the private cabinet of her son. His bust, nevertheless, is not a good likeness, nor is it agreeable. But it is a touching proof of the love of the widower. Is it not wonderful that simply by the force of this love a musician should have been transformed into a sculptor? This was M. de Beriot's only work in this line of art." Later, M. Cottinet, having seen a photograph of the mask, added: "It is she! The first moment I saw it I recognized it, with feelings of profound emotion and tender pity. It is she, with her slightly African type, containing, perhaps, a little negro blood (her father, Garcia, being of Spanish-Moorish descent). It is she as death found her, her face ruined by that terrible fall from her horse.... It is undoubtedly the mask from which her husband made the bust, which did not seem to be as charming as she was. Mr. Hutton may be perfectly satisfied that he possesses an authentic cast."

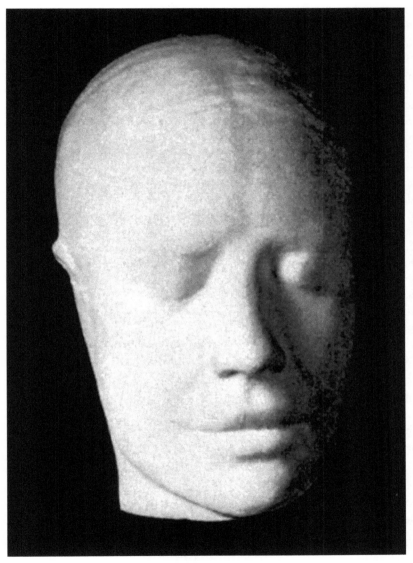

MARIA F. MALIBRAN

The head of Schiller has lain as uneasily since his death as if he had worn a crown, or, like Cromwell, had rejected one. The story of its posthumous wanderings is very grewsome. It is told at length by Emil Palleske in his *Life of Schiller*, and at greater length by Mr. Andrew Hamilton. The poet left a widow and family almost friendless and almost penniless; his brother-in-law Wolzogen was absent, and Goethe lay very ill. A cast of Schiller's head was taken by Klauer; and his body, hurriedly put into a plain deal coffin of the cheapest kind, was buried in a public vault, with nothing to designate whose body it was, and without the utterance of a word or a note of requiem. Twenty-one years later, as was the custom of the place, this public vault was emptied, and the bones it contained were scattered to make room for a new collection. Friends of Schiller, after great and unpleasant labor, gathered together twenty-three of these dishonored skulls, from which they selected as Schiller's that one "which differed enormously from all the rest in size and shape;" they compared it with Klauer's cast, and accepted its identity. It was then deposited, with no little ceremony, in the hollow pedestal containing Dannecker's colossal bust of Schiller in the Grand Ducal Library at Weimar. Goethe, however, desiring to recover more of the mortal part of his friend, had the head removed again and fitted to the rest of the bones of the body. These bones were deposited also in the Library, and the head put back in its pedestal. In 1827, at the suggestion of Louis of Bavaria, the head and the trunk were reunited and placed in a vault which the grand duke had built for himself and for his own family; and there, by the side of Goethe, who joined him in 1832, Schiller still rests.

Palleske, describing Schiller's death, says: "Suddenly an electric shock seemed to vibrate through him, the most perfect peace lit up his countenance, his features were those of one calmly sleeping." And this is the impression his death-mask gives.

Carlyle in one of his flash-light pictures thus photographed Schiller—the negative was found in the Commonplace-book of the late Lord Houghton—"He was a man with long red hair, aquiline nose, hollow cheeks, and covered with snuff."

A strange uneasiness seems to have possessed the bones of many of the great composers. Mozart's skull is said to be in the possession of Prof. Hyrtl, the famous anatomist of Vienna, who proposes to bequeath it to the Mozarteum at Salzburg. Mozart, like Schiller, was buried by an impoverished family in a grave unmarked save by a musical grave-digger, who secured the head—according to what seems to be very vague tradition—ten years later, and kept it, so long as he himself lived, in a cupboard in his humble lodgings in the precincts of the Cemetery of St. Marx. From him it passed to a second grave-digger, also musical, from whom it came into the possession of the Hyrtls. Those who have examined it, however, say that it has none of the peculiarities which, according to the existing theories of phrenology, should mark the presence of musical genius. And these peculiarities, strangely enough, are said to have been lacking in the skulls of Haydn, Schubert, and Beethoven, each of which, like the skulls of Mozart and Schiller and of Shakspere's Yorick, had a tongue in it, and could sing once; and each seems to have been knocked about the mazzard with a sexton's spade, and to have been used to point a moral, and, perhaps, even to stop a bunghole.

FREDERICK SCHILLER

Haydn's skull, it may be mentioned, is believed to be in the possession of the family of an eminent physician in Vienna. The rest of his body, originally buried in Hundsthurn church-yard, now lies in the parish church of Eisenstadt.

Beethoven's bones seem to have been disturbed but twice. His grave, in the Währing Cemetery at Vienna, having become almost uninhabitable from long neglect, he was reburied in the same spot in 1863; and in 1888 he was removed to the Central Cemetery of Vienna.

Beethoven's head is described, by those who knew him in life, as having been uncommonly large. His forehead was high and expanded. His eyes, when he laughed, seemed to sink into his head, although they were distended to an unusual degree when one of his musical ideas took possession of his mind. His mouth was well-formed; his under-lip protruded a little; his nose was rather broad. According to one authority "his skull [at the time of the exhumation in 1863] was discovered to be very compact throughout, and about an inch thick;" according to another authority it was "a small skull, and might have been supposed to belong to a man of restricted intellect, rather than to a genius like the great master."

Mr. Philip Hale, in *Famous Composers and their Works*, says: "The dimensions of the forehead were extraordinary; in height the forehead came next to that of Napoleon, and in breadth it surpassed it. His face was strong and sombre, and while it was not without ugliness it was expressive. The head was built stoutly throughout. The nose was thick, the jaw was broad, the mouth was firm and with protruding lips; the teeth were white, well-shaped, and sound, and when he laughed he showed them freely; the square chin rested on a white cravat. The greater number of pictures of Beethoven are idealized."

LUDWIG VON BEETHOVEN—From Life

LUDWIG VON BEETHOVEN—From Death

Beethoven's left ear-shell, it is said, is preserved in the cabinet of curiosities of a musical family in England. The mask of his face is one of the few casts of notable men to be found in the Museum of the British Phrenological Association in Ludgate Circus, London. It reposes, in plaster, in that institution, by the side of the cast of the head of Richard Brinsley Sheridan.

Two masks of Beethoven are in existence. The first was taken from life by Franz Klein in 1812, when the subject was in his forty-second year. Mr. Hale considers this "and the bust made after it by the same artist as of the first importance in forming a correct judgment of the value of all the portraits of Beethoven." The second mask was made by Dannhauser, on March 28, 1827, two days after Beethoven died. Both casts are here reproduced.

Beethoven was fond of telling the following story about himself. It will give a very fair idea of what he considered to be the size of his own cranium. Meeting the entire Imperial Family of Austria, on one occasion, at Töplitz, in the summer of 1812, "I pressed my hat down on my head," he said, "buttoned up my great-coat, and walked with folded arms through the thickest of the throng; princes and pages formed a line—the Archduke Rudolph took off his hat, and the Emperor made the first salutation. Those gentry know me!"

It is hardly to be wondered at that Goethe, who was his companion, should have been made very uncomfortable by the display of what looks like a piece of impertinence, even to republican eyes, and even at the end of three-quarters of a century of enlightenment. It is pleasant to read that royalty itself was highly amused by the whole performance.

Perhaps the best pen-picture of Mendelssohn in existence is that taken by Bayard Taylor, who wrote that "his eyes were dark, lustrous, and unfathomable. They were black, but without the usual opaqueness of black eyes; shining, not with a surface light, but with a pure serene planetary flame. His brow, white and unwrinkled, was high and nobly arched, with great breadth at the temples, and strongly resembling that of Poe. His nose had the Jewish prominence, without its usual coarseness; I remember particularly that the nostrils were as finely cut and as flexible as an Arab's. The lips were thin and rather long, but with an expression of undescribable sweetness in their delicate curves. His face was a long oval in form, and the complexion pale, but not pallid. As I looked upon him I said to myself—'The Prophet David!'"

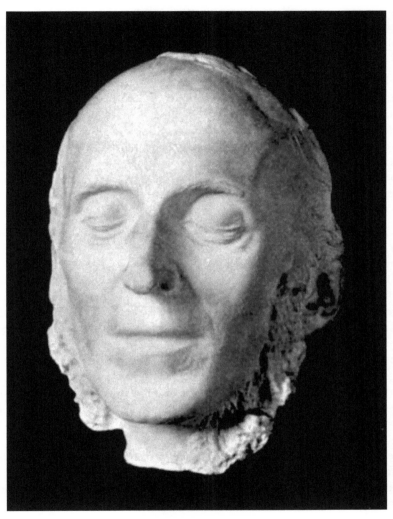

FELIX MENDELSSOHN

Lampadius, in his *Life of Mendelssohn*, said of the composer's death: "His features soon assumed an almost glorified expression. So much he looked like one in sleep that some of his friends thought that it could not be death, an illusion which is often given to the eye of love. His friends Bendemann and Hübner took a cast of his features as he lay."

A clever Frenchman said not long since, in the Paris *Gaulois*, that the Pantheon is nothing but a Grand Hotel, in which the distinguished guests find a temporary lodging-place, and then, like other transients, give up their rooms to somebody else. Mirabeau, Marat, Rousseau, and Voltaire boarded there for a time, and then surrendered their apartments, which are now occupied by Victor Hugo and a few men of no literary, artistic, or political importance; all of whom will, no doubt, in their turn, and before many years, be forced to find some second-class *pension*, where the rates are lower and the service is bad.

It was discovered lately that Mirabeau had again changed his quarters, and that his present address cannot be ascertained. He was carried in great pomp, and with many porters and in many 'busses, to the Pantheon, in 1791; but with Marat he was "de-Pantheonized by order of the National Convention" a year or two later. Marat's body was thrown into a common sewer in the Rue Montmartre; that of Mirabeau was placed, with no pomp whatever, in the cemetery of Saint-Marcel, the criminals' burying-ground, where, now that it is wanted once more—this time for honorable disposal—it cannot be found. Mirabeau's is the face of a man perfectly satisfied with his own achievements and with his own personal appearance. He believed, and he was courageous enough to say, that pure physical beauty in man could only exist in a face which was pitted with small-pox, his own being so marked! And he looks here as if his last thought in life had been one of profound admiration for himself. An eye-witness of his funeral said to one of his biographers that, "except a single trace of physical suffering, one perceived with emotion the most noble calm and the sweetest smile upon that face, which seemed enwrapped in a living sleep, and occupied with an agreeable dream."

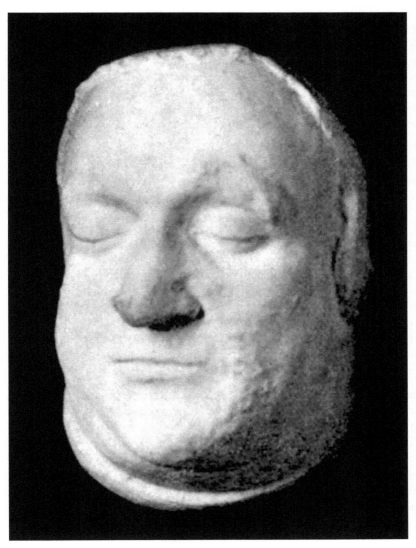

G. R. MIRABEAU

Marat and Robespierre are among the most enigmatical productions of a very enigmatical movement. During their lives they were not very beautiful in conduct nor very amiable in character; but the casts taken of their faces after their uncomfortable deaths are quiet and peaceful, and the effect they produce is one of loving rather than loathing. In the mask of each the cerebral development is small, especially in the region of the frontal bone; and phrenological experts who have examined them say that their development, or lack of development, taken with their facial traits, indicates ill-balanced minds.

Marat's face, as David painted him, is that of a North-American Indian with a white skin. The contemporary portraits of Robespierre, on the other hand, represent a mild-mannered man of severe and pensive expression. According to Lamartine, "his forehead was good, but small, and projecting over the temples, as if enlarged by the mass and embarrassed movements of his thoughts. His eyes, much veiled by their lids, and very sharp at the extremities, were deeply buried in the cavities of their orbits; they were of a soft blue color. His nose, straight and small, was very wide at the nostrils, which were high and too expanded. His mouth was large, his lips thin and disagreeably contracted at each corner, his chin small and pointed. His complexion was yellow and livid. The habitual expression of his face was the superficial serenity of a grave mind, and a smile wavering betwixt sarcasm and sweetness. There was *softness*, but of a sinister character. The dominant characteristic of his countenance was the prodigious and continued tension of brow, eyes, mouth, and all the facial muscles."

The masks of Mirabeau, Marat, and Robespierre are known to have been taken, in each case, after death, "by order of the National Assembly." Those of Marat and Robespierre in my collection are identical with the wax effigies in the "Chamber of Horrors" in Madame Tussaud's gallery in London, her catalogue asserting that they are "authentic;" and very fine casts of Mirabeau and Marat are in the Musée Carnavalet in Paris, the latter hanging under David's portrait of Marat, painted from nature immediately after the assassination.

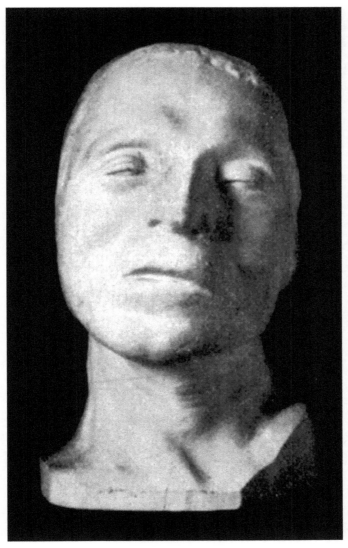

JEAN PAUL MARAT

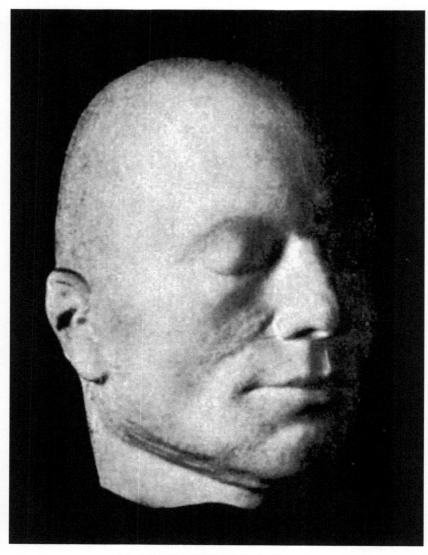

MAXIMILIAN ROBESPIERRE

The contemporaries of Sir Isaac Newton, like those of Kean, were all so much impressed by what he knew and by what he did, that they seldom thought of posterity as caring to know how he looked, either in life or in death. From many different sources, however, we learn, in a fragmentary way, that he was "short but well-set, and inclined to be corpulent;" that "he had a very lively and piercing eye;" that "his hair was abundant and white as silver, without any baldness, and when his peruke was off was a venerable sight;" that "he was a man of no very prominent aspect;" that "his face was almost square, and that his chin had unusual width;" that "although he reached the great age of eighty-four, he retained until the last almost all of his teeth;" and that "his countenance was mild, pleasant, and comely." Bishop Atterbury said, "in the whole air of his face and make there was nothing of that penetrating sagacity which appears in his compositions. He had something rather languid in his look and manner, which did not raise any very great expectation in those who did not know him;" and Dr. Humphrey Newton, who was his assistant and amanuensis, said that during the many years of their intimate association he never knew him to laugh but once!

His death was not without pain, and his mask will not be recognized readily by those who are familiar with his face as pictured and sculptured with his peruke on.

If Sir David Brewster's account of Newton's life be the true one, he was as good as he was great, and nothing can be added to that. His portraits by Lely, Kneller, and other famous painters still exist in different parts of Great Britain.

The terra-cotta bust of Newton, from the hand of Roubilliac, is in the British Museum. His bust and full-length statue in marble, by the same artist, belong to Trinity College, Cambridge. They were both, as is well known, based upon this mask of his face, taken after death, the original of which, made by Roubilliac, is now in the rooms of the Royal Society, at Burlington House in London. It was presented to that institution in 1829 by Samuel Hunter Christie, and the officers of the society have no doubt of its authenticity. Mr. Christie found it by accident in the shop of a dealer in statuary, whose father had purchased it at the sale of Roubilliac's effects more than half a century before. The dealer parted with it for a few shillings, although he was satisfied that it was the mask of Newton, and by Roubilliac. Charles Richard Weld, in his *History of the Royal Society*, gave a steel engraving of it, and declared that "it presents all the characteristic features of the Society's former illustrious president." Only a few copies of it are known to exist, and it is one of the most valuable and important masks in my collection.

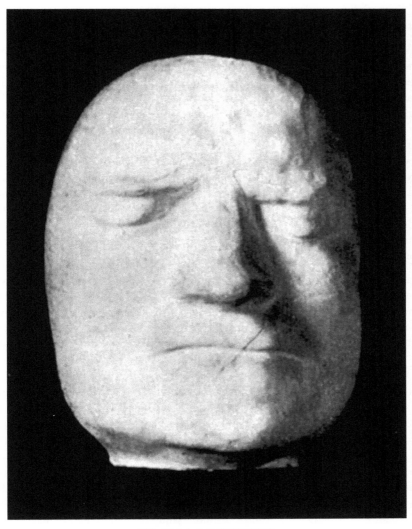

SIR ISAAC NEWTON

Roubilliac's mask of Alexander Pope was one of the cherished possessions of Samuel Rogers, but its present whereabouts I have not been able to discover.

The contrasts between the profoundest of England's philosophers and the bravest of her bruisers are as marked in an intellectual as in a physical way. Ben Caunt, the pugilist, died in London in 1861, universally respected. He was, during the later years of his life, proprietor of the Coach and Horses, a public-house in St. Martin's Lane, much frequented by his old pupils, and by all the prominent patrons of the prize-ring. He came to America in the early Forties, giving a series of exhibitions throughout the country, but never engaging in any serious encounter here. He was a leader in his own profession, and at one time, perhaps, the best-known man in all England. His portrait, which once adorned the walls of cottage and palace, is still to be found in Miles's *Pugilistica*, taken at the period of his famous fight with "Bendigo" in 1842. His head is certainly a strong one, and, in a phrenological way, he was better than many of the men among his contemporaries who did better things.

Thackeray, like most Anglo-Indian infants, was sent, when he was about five years of age, to the mother-country for mental and physical nourishment. An aunt, with whom he lived, discovered the child one morning parading about in his uncle's hat, which exactly fitted him. Fearing some abnormal and dangerous development of the brain, she carried him at once to a famous physician of the day, who is reported to have said, "Don't be afraid, madam; he has a large head, but there's a good deal in it!" How much was in it subsequent events have certainly proved. His brain, when he died, fifty-three years later, weighed fifty-eight and a half ounces. In 1849 or 1850, Charlotte Brontë wrote of Thackeray: "To me the broad brow seems to express intellect. Certain lines about the nose and cheek betray the satirist and cynic; the mouth indicates a childlike simplicity— perhaps even a degree of irresoluteness in consistency—weakness in short, but a weakness not unamiable." And Motley, writing to his wife in 1858, said: "I believe you have never seen Thackeray; he has the appearance of a colossal infant, smooth, white, shining ringlety hair, flaxen, alas! with advancing years; a roundish face, with a little dab of a nose, upon which it is a perpetual wonder how he keeps his spectacles." This broken nose was always a source of amusement to Thackeray himself; he caricatured it in his drawings, he frequently alluded to it in his speech and in his letters, and he was fond of repeating Douglas Jerrold's remark to him when he was to stand as godfather to a friend's son—"Lord, Thackeray, I hope you won't present the child with your own mug!"

BEN. CAUNT

WILLIAM MAKEPEACE THACKERAY

It is not pleasant to look upon the face of Thackeray—the face of which we love to think so pleasantly—as distorted by death. He was found dead in his bed on the morning of December 24, 1863:—"So young a man," as Dickens wrote, "that the mother who blessed him in his first sleep blessed him in his last. The final words he corrected in print," continued Dickens, "were—'And my heart throbbed with an exquisite bliss.' God grant that on that Christmas eve when he laid his head back on his pillow, and threw up his arms as he had been wont to do when very weary, some consciousness of duty done, and Christian hope throughout life humbly cherished, may have caused his heart so to throb when he passed away to his Redeemer's rest!" "And, lo," said Thackeray himself once, of the most beautiful character in all fiction, his own Thomas Newcome—"And, lo, he whose heart was as that of a little child had answered to his name, and stood in the presence of The Master!"

"We think of Thackeray," wrote Dr. John Brown, of Edinburgh, "as of our Chalmers, found dead in like manner: the same childlike, unspoiled, open face, the same gentle mouth, the same spaciousness and softness of nature, the same look of power. What a thing to think of—his lying there alone in the dark, in the midst of his own mighty London; his mother and his daughters asleep, and, it may be, dreaming of his goodness. Long years of sorrow, labor, and pain had killed him before his time. It was found after death how little life he had to live. He looked always fresh with that abounding silver hair, and his loving, almost infantile face; but he was worn to a shadow, and his hands wasted as if by eighty years."

The cast of Thackeray's face was made by Brucciani on that sad Christmas morning, at the request of Dr., now Sir, Henry Thompson; and a cast of his right hand was made at the same time—that honest, faithful, beautiful, wasted right hand, which

"never writ a flattery,

Nor signed the page that registered a lie."

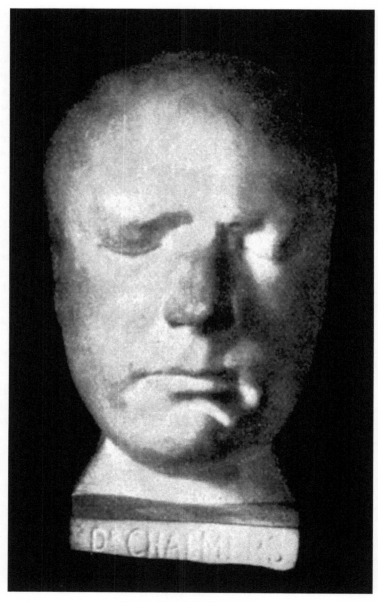

THOMAS CHALMERS

Thomas Chalmers was another man of great heart and of great head. He died, as we have seen, as Thackeray died, without warning, but without pain or conflict. He was discovered sitting half erect in his bed, his head reclining quietly on his pillow, the expression of his countenance that of fixed and majestic repose. He had responded cheerfully when his name was called. Thackeray heard the summons evidently in a moment of physical distress; but his "*Adsum*" was just as ready, and no doubt it was quite as willingly uttered.

"In height and breadth and in general configuration," wrote Julian Charles Young, "Dr. Chalmers was not unlike Coleridge. I have, since I knew Coleridge, sometimes thought that if Chalmers's head had been buried from sight, I could easily have mistaken him for that remarkable man. His face was pallid and pasty, and, I rather think, showed slight traces of small-pox. His features were ordinary; his hair was scanty, and generally roughed, as if his fingers had often passed through it; his brow was not high, but very broad, and well developed. His skull, phrenologically speaking, argued great mathematical power, but showed deficiency in the very qualities for which he was conspicuous, namely, benevolence and veneration."

Concerning Coleridge, Young wrote: "His general appearance would have led me to suppose him a dissenting minister. His hair was long, white, and neglected; his complexion was florid; his features were square; his eyes watery and hazy; his brow broad and massive; his build uncouth; his deportment grave and abstracted."

Charles Cowden Clarke, in his *Recollections*, spoke of Coleridge as "large-presenced, ample-countenanced, grand-foreheaded," and said that "the upper part of his face was excessively fine. His eyes were large, light gray, prominent, and of a liquid brilliancy. The lower part of his face was somewhat dragged, indicating the presence of habitual pain; but his forehead was prodigious, and like a smooth slab of alabaster." Leigh Hunt likened his brow to "a great piece of placid marble," and added that even in his old age "there was something invincibly young in the look of his face." "This boylike expression" he considered "very becoming in one who dreamed and speculated as Coleridge did when he was really a boy, and who passed his entire life apart from the rest of the world with a book and his flowers."

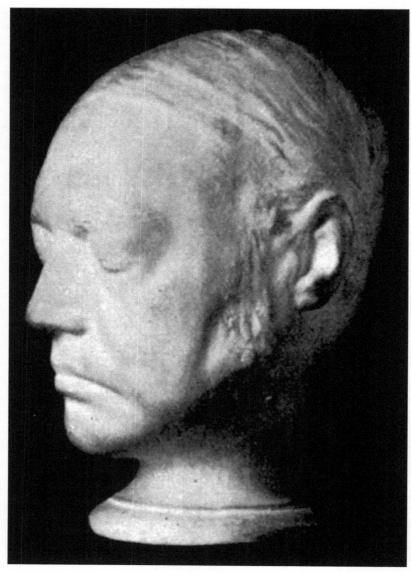

SAMUEL TAYLOR COLERIDGE

Carlyle's portrait of Coleridge is peculiarly in the Carlylian vein. "Figure a fat, flabby, incurvated personage, at once short, rotund, and relaxed; with a watery mouth; a snuffy nose; a pair of strange brown, timid, and yet earnest-looking eyes; a high tapering brow; and a great brush of gray hair—and you have some faint idea of Coleridge."

Coleridge himself was not more flattering to Coleridge. In 1796 he wrote to John Thelwall: "My face, unless when animated by immediate eloquence, expresses great sloth, and great, indeed almost idiotic, good-nature. 'Tis a mere carcass of a face, fat, flabby, and expressive chiefly of inexpression. Yet I am told that my eyes, eyebrows, and forehead are physiognomically good."

Mrs. Sara Coleridge, in her *Memoir*, gave a long account of Coleridge's death and burial, in which she said that "his body was opened, according to his own urgent request;" but, as usual in such cases, she did not allude to the making of any cast of his face or head.

Mr. Ernest Hartley Coleridge, however, the son of Derwent Coleridge, who is preparing a *Life* of his illustrious grandfather, writes, in a private note: "My mother used to tell me that the bust in her possession was by Spurzheim, and was taken from a death-mask; but with regard to Spurzheim, she must have been in error, as he died before Coleridge. Lord Coleridge says that the bust in *his* possession is by Spurzheim, and was taken from a cast of the poet's features; but whether he falls into the same error as my mother did, I cannot say. It is, of course, possible that Spurzheim took a life-cast from Coleridge's face."

Mr. Ernest Coleridge is inclined to accept the authenticity of the mask in my collection. It certainly bears a strong resemblance to the two busts of which he writes, as well as to the portrait by Allston, now in the National Portrait Gallery in London.

Carlyle said that "Wordsworth's face bore marks of much, not always peaceful, meditation; the look of it not bland or benevolent so much as close, impregnable, and hard." S. C. Hall wrote that "his eyes were mild and up-looking; his mouth coarse rather than refined; his forehead high rather than broad;" while Greville put it more tersely when he described him as "hard-featured, brown, wrinkled, with prominent teeth, and a few scattered gray hairs." Leigh Hunt said, in his *Autobiography*: "Certainly I never beheld eyes that looked so inspired or supernatural [as Wordsworth's]. They were like fires half burning, half smouldering, with a sort of acrid fixture of regard, and seated at the further end of two caverns. One might imagine Ezekiel or Isaiah to have had such eyes."

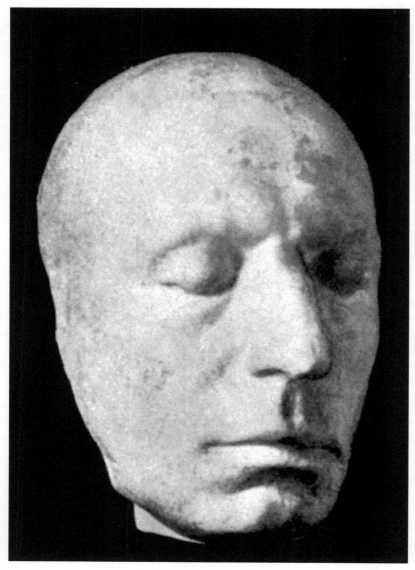

WILLIAM WORDSWORTH

Wordsworth reminded Hazlitt "of some of Holbein's heads—grave, saturnine, with a slight indication of sly humor, a peculiar sweetness in his smile." Elsewhere Hazlitt spoke of his "intense high, narrow forehead, Roman nose, cheeks furrowed by strong purpose, and a convulsive inclination to laughter about his mouth, which was a good deal at variance with the solemn and stately expression of the rest of his face." And Sir Humphry and Lady Davy, who were at Wordsworth's funeral, were both struck by the likeness of his face, in the deep repose of death, to that of Dante. The expression, they thought, was much more feminine than it had been in life, and it suggested strongly the face of his devoted sister, with whom so many of his years had been spent.

Haydon, in his *Journal*, April 13, 1815, wrote: "I had a cast made yesterday of Wordsworth's face. He bore it like a philosopher. He sat in my dressing-gown with his hands folded; sedate, solemn, and still." And then Haydon described how, through the open door, he exhibited the unconscious poet, undergoing this unbecoming operation, to curious but disrespectful friends of them both.

Another account of this performance shows us Wordsworth flat on his back on the studio floor, with Charles Lamb dancing about him, and making absurd remarks in order to force the poet to smile, and so spoil the mask. All of which was very characteristic of that "dear delightful," "poor creature" who was despised by Carlyle, and who was naturally loved by everybody else. What would we not give now for a mask of Lamb himself, dead or alive?

All this happened when Wordsworth was forty-two years of age, and thirty-five years before he died. Sir Henry Taylor in his *Autobiography*, spoke, shortly after the poet's death, of "a cast taken of a mask of Wordsworth." He considered it admirable as a likeness, and added that it was so regarded by Mrs. Wordsworth. He saw "a rough grandeur in it, with which, if it was to be converted into marble, posterity might be contented." But he does not say whether it was a life-mask or a death-mask, and he does not refer to the Haydon mask as such. In no other work, in no biography of Wordsworth, and in no account of his last hours, is any allusion to the mask to be found. The face here reproduced is, without question, that of Wordsworth. It suggests the Wordsworth of middle age; it strongly resembles the portraits painted by Haydon; it is much too young in form and expression for the senile Wordsworth of the well-known Fraser Gallery; and there is little doubt of its being the work of Haydon alluded to above. Haydon is known to have painted several portraits of Wordsworth, one of which exhibits him in a Byron collar and another shows him with eyes rolling in fine frenzy over the composition of a sonnet on one of Haydon's own pictures. Haydon also introduced Wordsworth as a devout disciple in his large work called "Christ's Entry into Jerusalem," painted in 1818.

Mr. John Gilmer Speed, in his *Memoirs of Keats*, presents an engraving of "John Keats from the Life-Mask of Haydon in 1818," and pronounces it the most satisfactory of the likenesses of Keats that he has seen. In no other of the *Lives* of Keats is any allusion made to this mask; it is not mentioned in any of the published letters to or from Keats, or in *The Correspondence and Table-Talk of Haydon*. Joseph Severn, shortly before he died, told Mr. Richard Watson Gilder that he *believed* the cast to have been the work of Haydon, and that he prized it as the most interesting, as it is the most real and accurate, portrait of his friend in existence; and through him were procured the few copies of it in this country, one of which is here reproduced. Mr. Gilder considers it much more agreeable than the death-mask must have been, for it not only escapes the haggardness of death, but there is even, so it seems to him, a suggestion of humorous patience in the expression of the mouth. "In this mask," he adds, "one has the authentic form and shape—the very stamp of the poet's visage." And he calls attention to the fact of its remarkable resemblance to more than one of the members of the Keats family whom he has met.

JOHN KEATS

Charles Cowden Clarke, who does not seem to have been aware of the existence of the mask, said that the best portrait of Keats is the first done by Severn himself, that which is engraved in Hunt's *Lord Byron and his Contemporaries*. Lord Houghton, in his *Life of Keats*, quoted the description given him by a lady (probably Mrs. B. W. Procter), who watched Keats in the Surrey Institute in London, listening to Hazlitt's course of Lectures on the British Poets, in the winter of 1817-18. "His countenance," she said, "lives in my mind as one of singular beauty and brightness; it had an expression as if it had been looking at some glorious sight. His mouth was full and less intellectual than his other features." Leigh Hunt drew his portrait more carefully. "Every feature was at once strongly cut and delicately alive. If there was any faulty expression, it was in the mouth, which was not without something of a character of pugnacity. The face was rather long than otherwise; the upper lip projected a little over the under; the chin was bold, the cheeks sunken; the eyes mellow and glowing, large, dark, and sensitive; his hair, of a brown color, was fine, and hung in natural ringlets. His head was a puzzle for the phrenologists, being remarkably small in the skull, a singularity which he had in common with Byron and Shelley, whose hats I could not get on."

Mr. William Sharp quotes a letter of Joseph Severn, written a day or two after the death of Keats, in which he said to Charles Armitage Brown, "Yesterday a gentleman came to cast the face, hand, and foot" of Keats. And on the 3d of April, 1821, John Taylor wrote to Severn from London for "the mask, hand, and foot." The later history of these interesting casts I have never been able to learn.

The original cast of the life-mask of Keats, made in Haydon's studio, and very much finer than any of the replicas of it, is in the possession of the National Portrait Gallery in London. It was given by Keats himself to his intimate friend John Hamilton Reynolds, just before Keats went abroad to die. Reynolds bequeathed it to his sister, Miss Charlotte Reynolds, by whom it was presented, with a clear pedigree, to the trustees of the National Portrait Gallery. This cast, with the mask of Cromwell, and a copy of the mask of Dr. Johnson, are, curiously enough, the only life-masks or death-masks in the institution in question.

The printed portraits of Johnson are very many. He himself said, once, of the painting by Trotter, "Well, thou art an ugly fellow; but still, I believe thou art like the original." George Kearsley wrote that "his face was capable of great expression, both in respect to intelligence and mildness, as all those can witness who have seen him in the flow of conversation, or under the influence of grateful feelings;" and Bishop Percy wrote,

"Johnson's countenance, when in good humor, was not disagreeable. His face clear, his complexion good, and his features not ill-formed; many ladies have thought he might not have been unattractive when young."

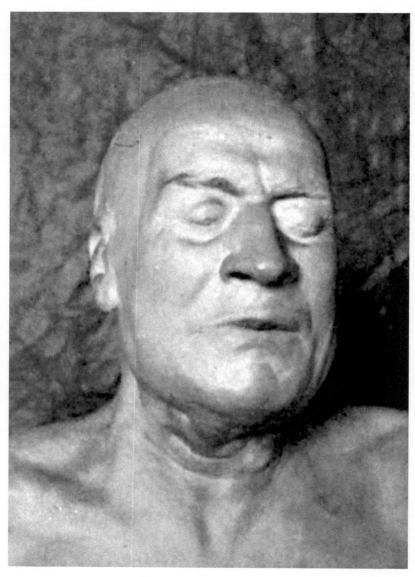

SAMUEL JOHNSON

The original of the mask of Johnson belongs to the Royal Literary Fund, the secretary of which, Mr. A. Llewellyn Roberts, in giving his consent to the reproduction of it here, writes as follows concerning it: "It was taken from a cast after death, under the direction of Dr. Johnson's medical attendant, Mr. Cruikshanks, who informed his daughter, into whose possession it came, that it was a remarkably correct likeness. Unfortunately there is no record of the artist's name, but it is alleged that each member of Dr. Johnson's family had a copy." This particular copy was given to the Royal Literary Fund by William Hutchins, who lived in Hanover Square. There is no reference to the taking of the mask of Johnson to be found in any of the editions of Boswell's *Life* of the great lexicographer.

Keats and Haydon first met in the house of Leigh Hunt in November, 1816, and to their mutual delight. They became very intimate upon very short acquaintance, and the poet was constantly to be found in the studio of the painter; they vowed that they were dearer to each other than brothers, and they prayed that their hearts might be buried together. Naturally a friendship so enthusiastic in its beginning did not last very long, and Haydon seems to have been most unjust in his reflections upon Keats, written some time after Keats's heart had been buried in Rome—and alone! Haydon wrote in the first flush of his intimacy with Keats: "Never have I had such irresistible and perpetual urgings of future greatness. I have been like a man with air-balloons under his arm-pits and ether in his soul; while I was painting, walking, or thinking, beaming flashes of energy followed and impressed me—they came over me, and shot across me, and shook me, till I lifted up my heart and thanked God."

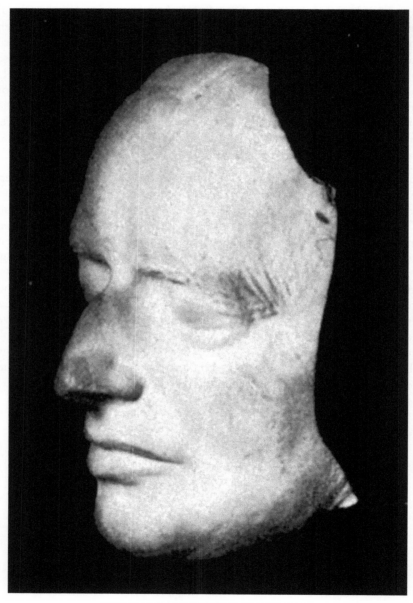

BENJAMIN ROBERT HAYDON

This is Haydon upon himself. Macaulay looked at him in a different light. "Haydon,"—he wrote in his *Diary* in 1853—"Haydon was exactly the vulgar idea of a man of genius. He had all of the morbid peculiarities which are supposed by fools to belong to intellectual superiority—eccentricity, jealousy, caprice, indefinite disdain for other men; and yet he was as poor, commonplace a creature as any in the world. He painted signs, and gave himself more airs than if he had painted the Cartoons. Whether you struck him or stroked him, starved him or fed him, he snapped at your hand in just the same way!"

In the *Memoir* of Haydon by his son is a fine engraving of the death-mask of Haydon, a replica of which is in my collection. This mask, with that of Jeremy Bentham, was broken, as you here see them, by careless Custom-house officers on their arrival in New York a few years ago.

James Parton quoted Burr as saying of Jeremy Bentham, "It is impossible to conceive a physiognomy more strongly marked with ingenuousness and philanthropy." John Stuart Mill said of him that "he was a boy till the last." And at the age of eighty-two he himself wrote to an old friend: "I am alive, though turned of eighty; still in good health and spirits; codifying like a dragon." "Candor in the countenance, mildness in the looks, serenity upon the brow, calmness in the language, coolness in the movements, imperturbability united with the keenest feeling:" such, according to Brissot de Warville, were the characteristics of Bentham.

Since St. Denis of France used to walk about with his head under his arm, or used to sit about with his head in his lap, in the third century of our Christian era, no *post-mortem* performance is more grotesque than that of Jeremy Bentham, who left his body by will to Dr. Southwood Smith. The legatee was instructed to dissect it, and to deliver lectures upon it to his medical students and to the public generally. After these anatomical demonstrations a skeleton was to be made, and was made, of the bones. Dr. Smith "endeavored to preserve the head untouched"—the words are his own—"merely drawing away the fluids by placing it under an air-pump over sulphuric acid. By this means the head was rendered as hard as the skulls of the New-Zealanders, but all expression, of course, was gone. Seeing this would not do for exhibition, I had a mould made in wax by a distinguished French artist, taken from David's bust, Pickersgill's picture, and my own ring. The artist succeeded in producing one of the most admirable likenesses ever seen. I then had the skeleton stuffed out to fit Bentham's own clothes, and this was likewise fitted to the trunk. The figure was placed seated on the chair in which he usually sat, one hand holding the walking-stick which was his constant companion when he went out, called by him 'Dapple.' The whole was enclosed in a mahogany case with glass doors." Bentham was wont to amuse himself in his boyish old age with the vision of his presiding, as it were, in proper person at meetings of his disciples, and he even used to anticipate his being wheeled to the top of the table on festive occasions!

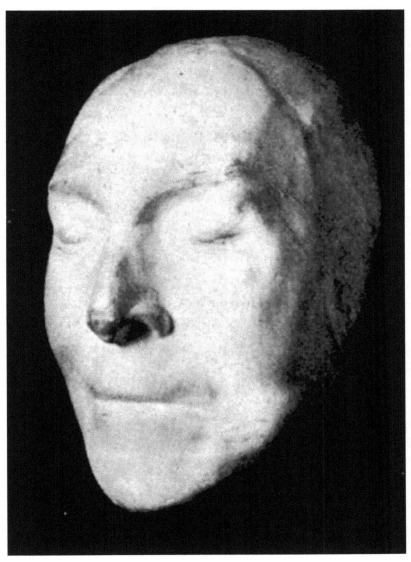

JEREMY BENTHAM

His figure as here described is still to be seen in the rooms of University College, Gower Street, London. It is curious that Dr. Smith did not go to the mask for a representation of Bentham's actual face. That such a mask was made, George Combe testified in the columns of the London *Phrenological Journal* a few years after Bentham's death. He said that it was in his own possession, and showed that "the knowing organ was large and the reflective organs only full." The mask, he said, was very like the portrait of Bentham reproduced in Tait's edition of Bentham's works. But he does not say whether it was a death-mask or the life-mask known to have been made by Turnerelli, an Italian sculptor living in London, in the early part of this century, and when Bentham was not more than fifty years of age. He was eighty-five when he died. This plaster mask of Bentham has been compared carefully with the wax effigy in University College. The mouth, the cranial arch, the entire upper part of the face, and the general shape of the head are very like, although in the wax mask the chin is shorter and rounder, and the eyes, of course, are open.

The mask of Rossetti was made by Brucciani, after death. Only three or four copies were cast, and the mould is in the possession of Mr. William M. Rossetti, through whose courtesy I am able to reproduce it here, and who writes: "I should say that my family and myself do not at all like the version of my brother's face presented by the mould and cast. In especial, singular though it may sound, the dimensions of the forehead seem wofully narrowed and belied. But of course, from a certain point of view, the cast tells truth of its own kind."

Mr. Hall Caine, writing of his own copy of the mask, says: "I ought perhaps to add that it does not give a good impression of Dante Rossetti. The upper part of the head is very noble, but the lower part is somewhat repellant."

A fourth copy belongs to Mr. George F. Watts, the painter, whose portrait of Rossetti is so well known.

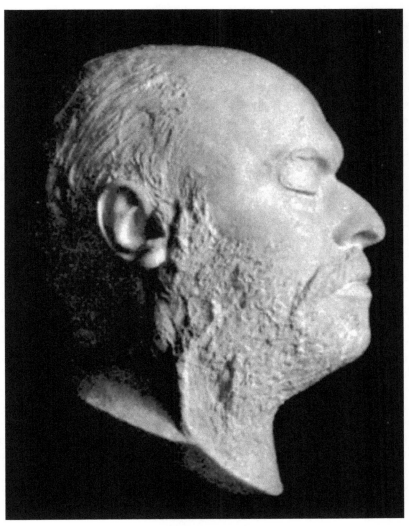

DANTE GABRIEL ROSSETTI

An anonymous writer in *Blackwood's Magazine* for January, 1893, who seems to have known Rossetti intimately, thus describes the head and front of the poet: "He was short, squat, bull-doggish; he belonged to the Cavour type, but the sallow face was massive and powerful. The impression of solidity is somewhat toned down in Watts's portrait, and the face is thinner and more worn than when I knew him. Sleepless nights and protracted pain may have changed him in later years and made the ideal Rossetti more manifest. Except for the meditative, tranquil eye (one thought of the ox-eyed Janus), there was nothing ideal about him. He was intensely Italian, indeed, but it was the sleek and well-fed citizen of Milan or Genoa that he recalled, not the slim and romantic hero of Verdi or Donizetti."

Cavour, according to George Eliot, who once got a glimpse of him in an Italian railway station, was a man pleasant to look upon, with a smile half kind and half caustic. He gave her the impression that "he thought of many matters, but thanked Heaven and made no boast of them." Elsewhere she said: "The pleasantest sight was Count Cavour in plainest dress, with a head full of power, mingled with *bonhomie*."

Mr. O. M. Spencer, in *Harper's Magazine* for August, 1871, devotes much space to the personal appearance of Cavour, who was, according to this authority, "of medium stature, with a tendency to corpulency; quick and energetic in his movements, with a forehead broad, high, and spacious; his eyes were partially closed by weakness and still further concealed by spectacles; his mouth not well formed and somewhat voluptuous, over which played an ironical smile, the joint offspring of mirth and disdain. Nevertheless, the *tout ensemble* of his countenance was expressive of benignity. Simple in his manners, though dignified in his bearing, he would have been recognized anywhere as a sub-alpine country gentleman, familiar with the usages of the court. Though of an irascible, phosphoric temperament, he rarely or never lost his self-control. Generous in his enmities and liberal in his friendships, he was chary of his confidence and exclusive in his intimacies. It may be that he was devoid of faith and affection, but he certainly loved Italy, and believed in his own mission."

The death-mask of Cavour, and that of Pius IX., I found lying peacefully side by side in a little plaster-shop in Rome in the autumn of 1893. The Pope was assuredly not devoid of faith and affection; and if he loved Italy less, it was only because he loved the Church of Rome more.

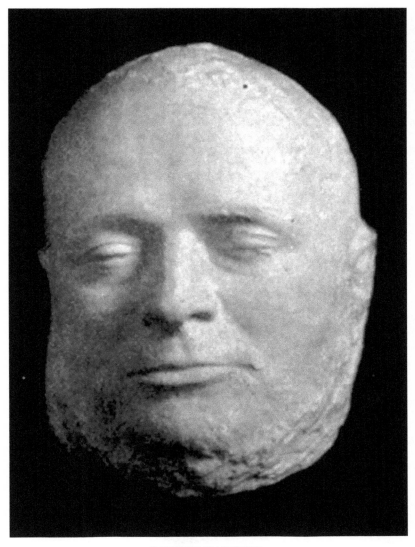

COUNT CAVOUR

PIUS IX.

Pius IX., we were told, at the time of his death in 1878, was a hale and vigorous septuagenarian, with a fine presence, a rich and melodious voice, a facile utterance, which rose at times to eloquence, and a benign countenance. For three days the body of the Pope lay in state in the Chapel of the Holy Sacrament in St. Peter's, and an eye-witness of the ceremonies wrote: "The face, perfectly visible, seemed unchanged from what it had been in life, and the expression was one of absolute peace; the calmness, indeed, was almost like that of sleep. A slight flush, even, was on the cheek, and a smile seemed to hover about the lips. The white hair peeped from under the mitre, and in the crossed hands, covered with red gloves, lay a crucifix suspended from a chain about his neck."

Signor A. Gallenza, in a volume entitled *The Pope and the King*, spoke of the pontiff's face in death as "handsome and dignified, with something like sternness in the lofty brow, strangely contrasting with that set smile so winning in the living man himself, but which was merely the result of a muscular contraction, a dimple which even death could not smooth."

Henry Crabb Robinson wrote from Italy in 1831: "I occasionally saw Leopardi, the poet, a man of acknowledged genius and of unimpeachable character. He was a man of good family and a scholar, but he had a feeble frame, was sickly and deformed."

Leopardi's life was very unhappy. His bodily infirmities humiliated him, and domestic trials greatly affected his spirit. He seems to have inspired very little tenderness even in the heart of his own mother, and he died as miserably as he lived, longing for the eternal rest from pain and neglect. His contemporaries have left almost nothing on record concerning his personal appearance, but the few existing portraits of him, and particularly this cast of his dead face, certainly show sweetness mingled with strength. Mr. Howells, in his *Modern Italian Poets*, quotes Niebuhr as saying of the young Leopardi: "Conceive of my astonishment, when I saw standing before me, in the poor little chamber, a mere youth, pale and shy, frail in person and obviously in ill-health, who was by far the first, in fact the only, Greek philologist in Italy."

GIACOMO LEOPARDI

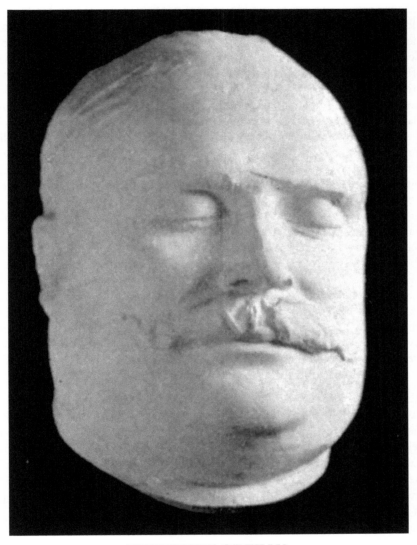

JOHN BOYLE O'REILLY

The best and most sympathetic portrait of John Boyle O'Reilly is the following, to be found in the life of that gentleman written by his friend, Mr. James Jeffrey Roche: "Recalling him as he then was [1870], the abiding memory of him is that of his marvellously sweet smile, and his strikingly clear and frank gaze; the beauty of his face lay chiefly in his eyes. The official advertisement of his escape says that those eyes were brown, and prison descriptions are generally more accurate than flattering. Almost anybody looking at him less closely, would have said that his eyes were black. As a matter of fact, they were hazel, but his dark skin and jet-black eyebrows and hair gave an impression of blackness to the large, well-formed eyes beneath. They were very expressive, whether flashing with some sudden fancy or glowing with a deeper burning thought, or sparkling with pure boyish fun. There was another expression, which they sometimes wore at this period of his life, and which may be described for lack of a better word, as a hunted look—not frightened or furtive, but an alert, watchful expression, which made it easy to understand how he could have deliberately armed himself with the firm intention of surrendering his liberty only with his life.... No portrait ever made of him does justice to that which was the great charm of his countenance—its wonderful light and life. His eyes had the depth and fire and mobile color of glowing carbuncle. For the rest he had the rich brown complexion, so familiar in after-years; a small black mustache, only half concealing his finely-cut mouth, and revealing a set of perfectly white, regular teeth. His form was slight, but erect and soldier-like. He carried his head well raised, and a little thrown back. He was a man whom no one would pass without a second glance."

It is rather a curious fact that the men most interested, naturally, in the study of the human face, and in its portrayal with chisel or pencil, are the men most poorly represented in this collection; Sir Thomas Lawrence being the only painter of portraits, and Hiram Powers, Haydon, and Canova the only makers of masks, whose masks are here presented. Three views of the life-mask of Sir Thomas Lawrence were engraved by R. J. Lane, in 1830. They are contained on one plate, and represent the full face, as well as profiles looking to the right and to the left. The print is very rare, and bears the following inscription: "From a plaster cast taken at the age of thirty-four, in the possession of an attached friend."

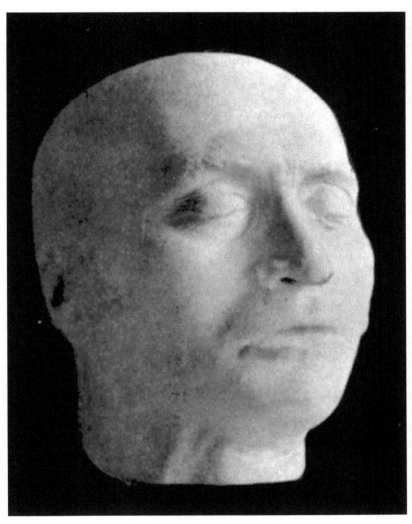

SIR THOMAS LAWRENCE

Edward H. Baily, the sculptor, is known to have made a cast of Lawrence's features after death. "The head was finely shaped and bald, and it bore a striking resemblance to that of Canning, although the face lacked something of Canning's elevated expression." This death-mask is here presented.

Lawrence is said to have been a beautiful creature in his boyhood, with bright eyes, and long chestnut hair. In later life we are told that "although not tall—he was under five feet nine inches—his beautiful face, active figure, agreeable manners, and fine voice were not thrown away upon either lords or ladies, emperors or kings." Opie said of him once, "Lawrence made coxcombs of his sitters, and his sitters made a coxcomb of him." And George IV., the Sir Hubert Stanley of fine manners, pronounced him "a high-bred gentleman." This is praise indeed! Another, and perhaps not so exalted an authority, said, "Lawrence's appearance was exceedingly graceful and gentlemanly. His countenance was open and noble, his eyes were large and lustrous and very expressive." Dr. R. R. Madden, in his *Memoirs of the Countess of Blessington*, quotes a brother artist, and a friend of Lawrence, as saying of him, "As a man Sir Thomas Lawrence was amiable, kind, generous, and forgiving. His manner was elegant but not high-bred. He had too much the air of always submitting. He had smiled so often, and so long, that at last his smile had the appearance of being set in enamel."

The mask of J. M. W. Turner formerly belonged to the late Dr. Pocock of Brighton, England, and is now in the possession of Mr. William Ward, of London. It was made, after death, by the late Thomas Woolner. There are but few portraits of Turner in existence, the most life-like being an engraving by M. M. Halloway, of a half-length profile sketch bearing this inscription: "Drawn by me in the print-room of the British Museum. J. T. Smith." Unfortunately no date is attached.

Much has been put on record about Turner's personal peculiarities and eccentricities; but little has been said by his contemporaries concerning his personal appearance. The best picture, although a slight one, is from the pen of Mr. W. P. Frith: "Turner was a very short man, with a large head, and a face usually much muffled to protect it from the draughts for which the rooms [of the Royal Academy] were celebrated."

J. M. W. TURNER

Cyrus Redding, in his *Past Celebrities*, speaks of Turner's "unprepossessing exterior, his reserve, and his austerity of language." Wilkie Collins once described him as seated on the top of a flight of steps, astride of a box, on Varnishing Day at the Royal Academy, "a shabby Bacchus, nodding like a mandarin at his picture, which he with a pendulum-motion now touched with his brush, now receded from." And Peter Cunningham, in an almost brutal way, set down Turner as "short, stout, and bandy-legged, with a red, pimply face, imperious and covetous eyes, and a tongue which expressed his sentiments with murmuring reluctance." Sir William Allen, according to Cunningham, was accustomed to describe the great painter as a "Dutch Skipper."

In view of all this, it is not remarkable that Turner had strong objections to sitting for his portrait. He felt that any familiarity with his face and figure would affect the poetry of his works in the popular mind. "No one," he said, "would believe, after seeing my likeness, that I painted these pictures." A contemporary portrait of Turner, fishing in all his uncouth enthusiasm, with shabby garments, and a cotton umbrella over his head, is unfortunately too long to be quoted here.

Hiram Powers died in Florence in 1873, and lies in the Protestant Cemetery of that city. His mask, after death, was made by Thomas Ball and Joel T. Hart. Dr. Samuel Osgood said of Powers in 1870: "In his looks, his ideas, as well as in all his works, he is a man of the golden mean. There is nothing too much in his make or his manner. He is a good specimen of a well-formed man, and his own statue would make a good sign for the front of his studio." In October, 1847, Mrs. Browning wrote: "Mr. Powers, the sculptor, is our chief friend and favorite. A most charming, simple, straightforward, genial American—as simple as the man of genius he has proved himself to be.... The sculptor has eyes like a wild Indian's, so black and full of light—you would scarcely marvel if they clove the marble without the help of his hand." "Mr. Powers called in the evening," wrote Hawthorne in his *Italian Note-book* in 1858—"a plain personage, characterized by strong simplicity and warm kindliness, with an impending brow, and large eyes which kindle as he speaks. He is gray and slightly bald, but does not seem elderly nor past his prime. I accept him at once as an honest and trustworthy man, and shall not vary from this judgment."

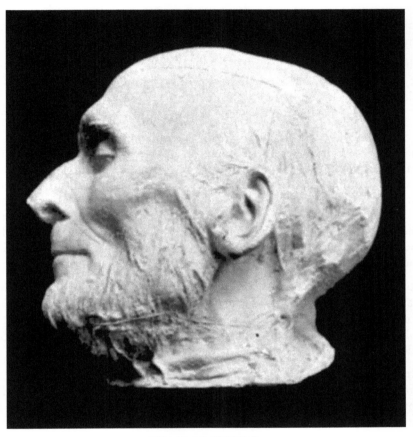

HIRAM POWERS

Mr. Preston Powers, who possesses the mask of his father, has also in his possession a life-mask and a death-mask of Agassiz, and a death-mask of Sumner; the last two having been made by himself. Through his courtesy I am enabled to reproduce them all here.

The life-mask of Agassiz was made when the subject was about forty years of age, and by an artist now unknown. It was given to Mr. Powers by Mr. Alexander Agassiz at the time of the elder Agassiz's death.

E. P. Whipple, in his *Recollections of Eminent Men,* said of Agassiz: "You could not look at him without feeling that you were in the presence of a magnificent specimen of physical, mental, and moral manhood; that in him was realized Sainte-Beuve's ideal of a scientist—the soul of a sage in the body of an athlete. At that time [1845] he was one of the comeliest of men. His full and ruddy face, glowing with health and animation, was crowned by a brow which seemed to be the fit home for such a comprehensive intelligence." And Longfellow, in his *Journal* (January 9, 1847), wrote: "In the evening a reunion at Felton's to meet Mr. Agassiz, the Swiss geologist and naturalist. A pleasant, voluble man, with a bright beaming face."

Mr. Curtis, in an oration upon Charles Sumner, delivered shortly after the statesman's death, said that "his look, his walk, his dress, his manner, were not those of the busy advocate, even in his younger years, but of the cultivated and brilliant man of society, the Admirable Crichton of the saloons."

Mrs. Jefferson Davis, in her *Life* of her husband, spoke of Sumner as "a handsome, unpleasing man, and an athlete whose physique proclaimed his physical strength." And Mr. Seward wrote to his wife in 1856: "Sumner is much changed for the worse. His elasticity and vigor are gone. He walks, and in every way moves, like a man who has not altogether recovered from a paralysis, or like a man whose sight is dimmed, and his limbs stiffened with age."

At the autopsy it was discovered that the brain of Sumner showed no trace of the assault from the effects of which he suffered so terribly.

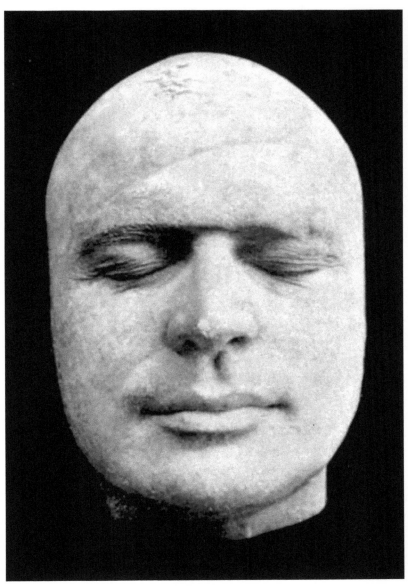

LOUIS AGASSIZ—From Life

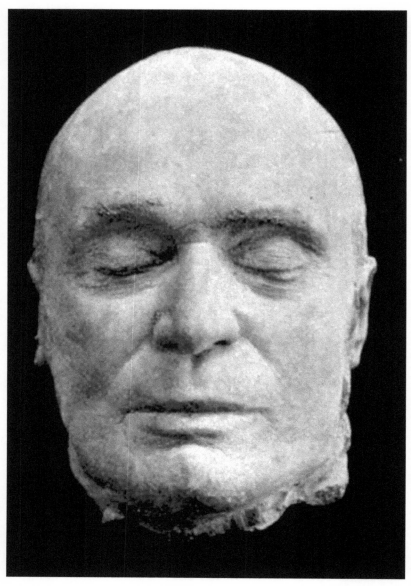

LOUIS AGASSIZ—From Death

CHARLES SUMNER

Canova must have been a beautiful character. It is not often that so much good is spoken, even of the dead, as has been spoken of him since he died; and if the chroniclers are right, he deserved it all. In personal appearance, however, we read that he was not particularly attractive. His hair was black and luxuriant, and his forehead of noble dimensions, but the outline of his features was neither grand nor extraordinary. The phrenologists gave him a massive brain upward and forward of the ears, wonderful constructive talent, with large ideality and strong intellect. He was very abstemious in his habits, very thoughtful, and a hard worker. Count Cicognara, in a biographical sketch of Canova, thus described his face during his very last hours: "His visage became, and remained for some time, highly radiant and expressive, as if his mind was absorbed in some sublime conception, creating powerful and unusual emotion in all around him. Thus he must have looked when imagining that venerable figure of the pontiff who is represented in the attitude of prayer in the Vatican. His death was wholly unattended by the agonies which make a death-bed so distressing, nor did even a sigh or convulsion announce his dying moment."

This is the visage which his friends cast in plaster, and it was, no doubt, the basis of the medallion bust of Canova, in profile, which forms part of the pyramidal tomb erected by certain of his pupils in 1827, in the church of Sante Maria Gloriosa dei Frari, the pantheon of Venice. The monument, according to Mr. Ruskin, is "consummate in science, intolerable in affectation, ridiculous in conception; null and void to the uttermost in invention and feeling;" and the medallion represents the great sculptor in all his glorious prime of strength and beauty.

The death-mask of Canova, as here reproduced, in its peaceful and quiet repose, is in strong contrast with that of Richard Brinsley Sheridan, shown upon a subsequent page.

ANTONIO CANOVA

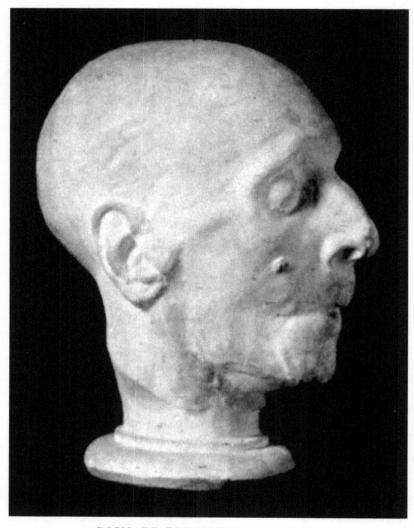

RICHARD BRINSLEY SHERIDAN

In the whole history of English letters, there can be found no sadder chapter than that which contains the story of Sheridan's death. The body out of which the breath was fast going, and from which intelligent action had entirely gone, was seized by sheriff's officers for debt, and only by the threats of attending physicians did it escape being carried to a low sponging-house, wrapped in nothing but the blankets that covered the bed on which it lay. The "life and succor" his friends had begged were denied him, and "Westminster Abbey and a funeral" were all he received. As a French journal said at the time, it only proved that "France is the place for a man of letters to live in, and England the place for him to die in." Sheridan's appearance during his last hours was thus depicted by one who saw for himself the havoc made: "His countenance was distorted under the writhings of unutterable anguish. Pain and the effects of pain were visible on that sunken cheek; and on that brow which had never knitted under oppression, or frowned upon the importunities of the unfortunate, pain in its most acute form had contracted there its harsh and forbidding lines.... Still, amid those rigid lines which continuous suffering had indented there, you might perceive the softer and more harmonious tracings of uncomplaining patience, fortitude in its endurance, and resignation in its calmness." This is the face exhibited here—one of the most unpleasant to look upon which the collection contains, notwithstanding Sheridan's own boast, not very long before his death, that "his eyes would look up as brightly at his coffin-lid as ever." His spirits did not fail him so long as consciousness remained, and when asked by the attending surgeons if he had ever before undergone an operation, he replied, "Only when sitting for my portrait, or having my hair cut." It is to be regretted that this last portrait for which he sat, should be so worn and weary in its expression. Moore, in his *Life of Sheridan*, did not mention the taking of the mask, although he spoke of the plaster cast of Sheridan's hand, under which some keen observer had written:

"Good at a fight, better at a play,

God-like in giving—but the devil to pay."

Concerning Moore's own appearance, Leigh Hunt wrote: "Moore's forehead was bony and full of character, with 'bumps' of wit large and radiant enough to transport a phrenologist. His eyes were as dark and fine as you would wish to see under a set of vine leaves; his mouth generous, and good-humored with dimples." Scott said in his *Journal*, in 1825: "Moore's countenance is plain, but the expression is very animated, especially in speaking or singing, so that it is far more interesting than the finest features could have rendered it." In 1833 Gerald Griffin made a visit to Moore at Sloperton, and thus described Moore himself: "A little man, but full of spirits, with eyes, hands, feet, and frame forever in motion.... I am no great observer of proportions, but he seemed to me to be a neat-made little fellow, tidily buttoned up, young as fifteen at heart, though with hair that reminded me of 'Alps in the sunset'; not handsome, perhaps, but something in the whole cut of him that pleased me."

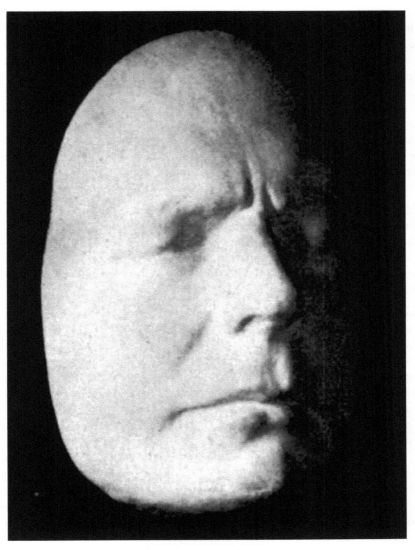

THOMAS MOORE

A year later, N. P. Willis, who *was* a great observer of proportions, met Moore at Lady Blessington's, and thus recorded his observations: "His forehead is wrinkled, with the exception of a most prominent development of the organ of gayety, which, singularly enough, shines with the lustre and smooth polish of a pearl, and is surrounded by a semicircle of lines drawn close about it like intrenchments against Time. His eyes still sparkle like a champagne bubble, though the invader has drawn his pencillings about the corners.... His mouth is the most characteristic feature of all. The lips are delicately cut, slight, and changeable as an aspen, but there is a set look about the lower lip—a determination of the muscle to a particular expression, and you fancy that you can almost see wit astride upon it.... The slightly tossed nose confirms the fun of the expression, and altogether it is a face that sparkles, beams, radiates."

This was Moore as others saw him when he was in his prime. His later years were clouded by a loss of memory, and a helplessness almost childish. The light of his intellect grew dim by degrees, although Lord John Russell said that there was never a total extinction of the bright flame. He died calmly and without pain; and the cast of his face certainly reflects much that Willis had drawn in his *Pencillings by the Way*.

Sheridan said once of a fellow-Irishman that Burke's "abilities, happily for the glory of our age, are not intrusted to the perishable eloquence of the day, but will live to be the admiration of that hour when all of us shall be mute, and most of us forgotten." Burke, in all his relations, was a better man than Sheridan, and he met, as he deserved, a better fate. He fell asleep for the last time with Addison's chapter on "The Immortality of the Soul" under his pillow, and with the respect and gratitude of all England at his feet. The mask of Burke was offered for sale—and was sold—in London a few months ago, with a certificate from Mr. Edward B. Wood, stating that it was made by the especial desire of Queen Charlotte on the day of Burke's death. The name of the artist is unknown, but he is said to have received two hundred guineas for the work. After the death of her Majesty the mask was given by George IV. to C. Nugent, his gentleman-in-waiting, from whom it came into the possession of his nephew, Mr. Wood. This original mask, from the Queen's cabinet, is now the property of The Players. It is very like the familiar portrait of Burke by Opie.

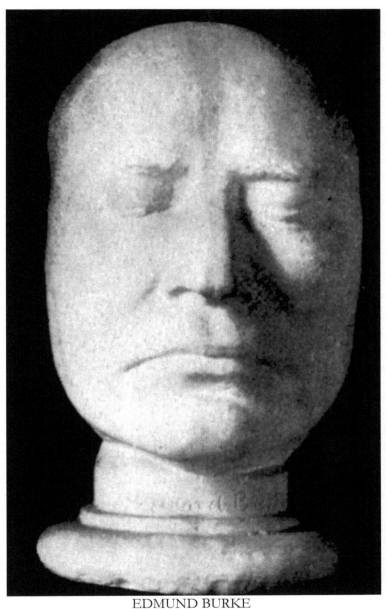

EDMUND BURKE

George Combe had a mask of Curran in this country, of which mine, no doubt, is a replica, as it bears a strong resemblance to the established portraits of Curran. Its existence does not appear to have been known to the sculptor of the medallion head of Curran on the monument in St. Patrick's, Dublin, for that was avowedly taken from the portrait by Sir Thomas Lawrence. A short time before his death Curran wrote to a friend that his "entire life had been passed in a wretched futurity," but that happily he had found the remedy, and that was to "give over the folly of breathing at all." He ceased to breathe at all in Brompton, London, in the autumn of 1817; and his bones, now buried in Dublin, were laid for some years in a vault of Paddington church.

We learn from various sources that Curran was under the middle height, "very ugly," with intensely bright, black eyes, perfectly straight jet-black hair, a "thick" complexion, and "a protruding underlip on a retreating face." Croker, speaking of his oratory, said: "You began by being prejudiced against him by his bad character and ill-looking appearance, like the devil with his tail cut off, and you were at last carried away by his splendid language and by the power of his metaphor."

The mask of Lord Palmerston was taken immediately after death at Brockton Hall, by Mr. Jackson. Only one cast was ever made—that which is in my collection—and upon this was based the head upon the statue of Palmerston by Mr. Jackson, now in Westminster Abbey. The Marquis of Lorne, in his *Life of Palmerston*, says: "Some of us may have seen him rise quickly and lightly, when nearly fourscore, from his seat in the House of Commons, and speak with clearness and directness but no attempt at eloquence, and often with some hesitation, at the table; his black frock-coat buttoned across the well-knit and erect figure of middle stature, his sentences spoken towards the bar of the House; his gray short hair brushed forward and the gray whiskers framing the head erect on the shoulders. Some may remember, under the shaven chin, the loose bow-knot, neatly tied at the throat, the bit of open shirt-front, with standing collar." His appearance in 1837 is thus described: "Lord Palmerston is tall and handsome. His face is round and of the darkest hue. His hair is black, and always exhibits proofs of the skill and attention of the *friseur*. His clothes are in the extreme of fashion. He is very fond of his personal appearance." And Sir William Fraser sketched him as he appeared to a later generation: "Lord Palmerston on horseback looked a big man, and standing at the table of the House he did not appear ill-proportioned. Each foot, to describe it mathematically, was 'a four-sided, irregular figure.' His portraits in *Punch* are very like him. Those with a flower or straw in the mouth are the best. He had a very horsy look."

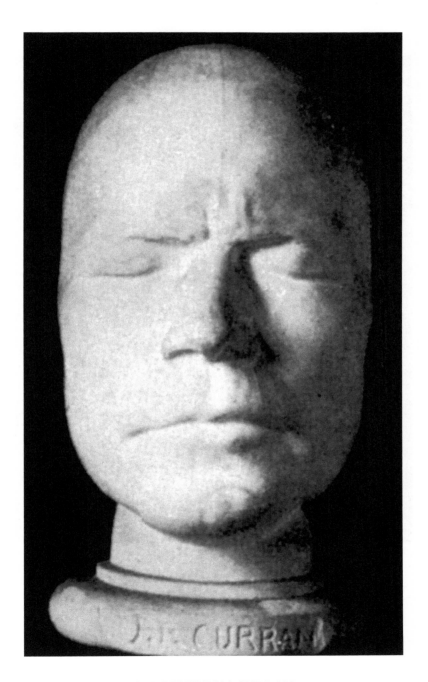

JOHN PHILPOT CURRAN

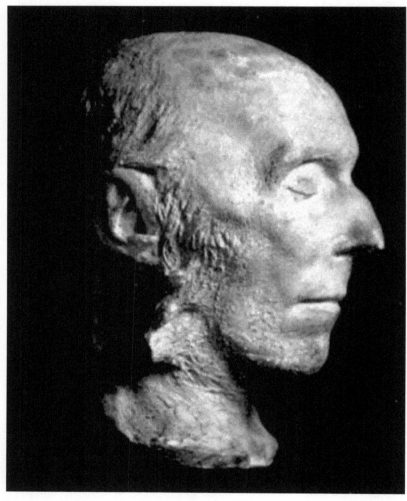

LORD PALMERSTON

The death-mask of Benjamin Disraeli, Earl of Beaconsfield, as here shown, was found by me a year or two ago in the out-of-the-way little shop of a mould-maker in Chelsea. It was taken by Sir Edgar Boehm, and the nose in the cast was broken, evidently intentionally and wantonly, by some malicious person who wished, perhaps, in this iconoclastic way to express with emphasis his political opinions. Despite its mutilated condition it is of great interest to all lovers and admirers of the original.

The best pen-portrait of Disraeli as well as the most familiar, is that of N. P. Willis, who saw him, in his youth, at Lady Blessington's. It says: "He was sitting in a window looking on Hyde Park, the last rays of sunlight reflected from the gorgeous gold flowers of a splendidly embroidered waistcoat. Patent-leather pumps, a white stick with a black cord and tassel, and a quantity of chain about his neck and pockets, served to make him a conspicuous object. He has one of the most remarkable faces I ever saw. He is lividly pale, and but for the energy of his action and the strength of his lungs, would seem to be a victim of consumption. His eye is as black as Erebus and has the most mocking, lying-in-wait sort of expression conceivable. His mouth is alive with a kind of working and impatient nervousness; and when he has burst forth, as he does constantly, with a particularly successful cataract of expression, it assumes a curl of triumphant scorn that would be worthy of Mephistopheles. His hair is as extraordinary as his taste in waistcoats. A thick, heavy mass of jet-black ringlets falls on his left cheek almost to his collarless stock, which on the left temple is parted and put away with the smooth carefulness of a girl. The conversation turned upon Beckford. I might as well attempt to gather up the foam of the sea as to convey an idea of the extraordinary language in which he clothed his description. He talked like a race-horse approaching the winning-post, every muscle in action." This is the Disraeli whom D'Orsay drew.

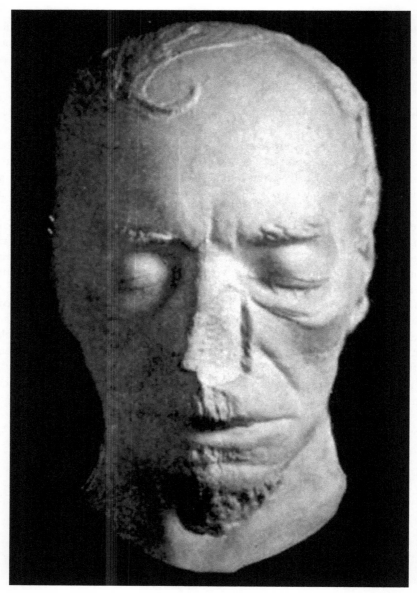

BENJAMIN DISRAELI

Mr. T. Wemyss Reid thus sketches Disraeli in later life: "Over the high arched forehead—surely the forehead of a poet—there hangs from the crown of the head a single curl of dark hair, a curl which you cannot look at without feeling a touch of pathos in your inmost heart, for it is the only thing about the worn and silent man reminding you of the brilliant youth of *Vivian Grey*. The face below this solitary lock is deeply marked with the furrows left by care's ploughshare; the fine dark eyes look downward, the mouth is closed with a firmness that says more for his tenacity of will than pages of eulogy would do; but what strikes you more than anything else is the utter lack of expression upon the countenance. No one looking at the face, though but for a moment, could fall into the error of supposing that expression and intelligence are not there; they are there, but in concealment."

Mr. W. P. Frith, in his *Autobiography*, more than once alludes to the devotion of Mrs. Disraeli to her husband, and he quotes John Phillips as describing the painting of Disraeli's portrait. After the subject and his wife had seen the sketch, during the first sitting, the colors being necessarily crude, the lady returned hastily to the studio, and said to the painter: "Remember that his pallor is his beauty!"

Dr. Wilde, afterwards Sir William Wilde, published in Dublin, in 1849, a volume entitled *The Closing Years of Dean Swift's Life*, a very interesting book now long out of print. It is an elaborate defence of Swift's sanity, and it contains a full account of the plaster mask taken from the Dean's face "after the *post-mortem* examination." From this, he said, "a bust was made and placed in the museum of the University, which, notwithstanding its possessing much of the cadaverous appearance, is, we are strongly inclined to believe, the best likeness of Swift—during, at least, the last few years of his life—now in existence." Speaking of this mask, Sir Walter Scott wrote: "The expression of countenance is most unequivocally maniacal, and one side of the mouth (the left) horribly contorted downwards, as if convulsed by pain." Dr. Wilde, on the other hand, said: "The expression is remarkably placid; but there is an evident drag in the left side of the mouth, exhibiting a paralysis of the facial muscles of the right side, which, we have reason to believe, existed for some years before his death."

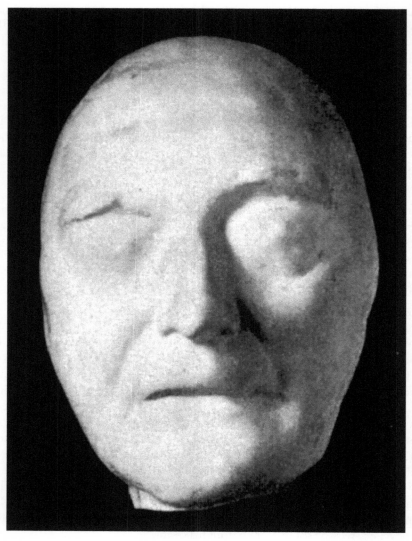

JONATHAN SWIFT

Dr. Wilde compared this cast of Swift's face, taken immediately after death, with the cast and drawings of his skull made in 1835, ninety years later, when the bodies of Swift and Stella were exhumed, and their craniums examined by the phrenologists belonging to the British Association; and by careful analysis of both, he was able to satisfy himself that Swift was not "a driveller and a show" when he died, nor a madman while he lived. He gave, upon the sixty-second page of his book, a drawing of this mask in profile, and the face is certainly identical with the face in my collection. It resembles very strongly the accepted portraits of Swift, particularly the two in which he was drawn without his wig. The more familiar of these is a profile in crayon, by Barber, taken when the Dean was about sixty years of age—and eighteen years before his death—which has been frequently engraved for the several editions of Lord Orrery's *Remarks on the Life and Writings of Jonathan Swift*, first published in 1751. The original cast was made in two parts, according to Dr. Wilde, and the difference in surface between the rough hinder part—not existing in my copy—and the smooth polished anterior portion, as here seen, shows at once that the back of the head was added at a later date. Two lines of writing, greatly defaced, found upon the cast attest this to be "Dean Swift taken off his ... the night of his burial, and the ... one side larger than the other in nature." In a foot-note to the second edition of his work, Dr. Wilde said: "The original mask remained in the museum T.C.D. [Trinity College, Dublin] till within a few years ago [1849], when it was accidentally destroyed." The history of this replica—for replica it certainly is—before it came into my hands I have never been able to trace. It found its way into the shop of a dealer in curiosities, who knew nothing of its pedigree, not even whose face it was; and from him I bought it for a few shillings. It is one of the most interesting of the collection, and perhaps the most valuable, because the most rare. It is hardly the Swift of our imagination, the man whom Stella worshipped and Vanessa adored; and, Dr. Wilde to the contrary, notwithstanding, one cannot help feeling while looking at it that Swift's own sad prophecy to Dr. Young was fulfilled—"I shall be like that lofty elm whose head has been blasted; I shall die first at the top."

At least one of the biographers of the Irish dean died as Byron often feared to die, "like Swift, at the top first." Sir Walter Scott's decay was a mental decay in the beginning of his last illness; but happily for him, and for his family, the axe was laid at the root of the grand old monarch of the forest of Scottish letters before the upper branches were permitted to go to utter ruin.

There exist at Abbotsford two masks of its first laird—a life-mask and a death-mask. Of the former very little is known except that it is said to have been made in Paris. The latter was exhibited at the Scott Centenary Celebration in Edinburgh, in 1871, when it attracted a great deal of attention. They both show, as no portrait of the living man shows, except the familiar sketch by Maclise in the Fraser Gallery, the peculiar formation of his head, and the unusual length above the eyes. Lockhart, in his account of Scott's last hours, said: "It was a beautiful day; so warm that every window was wide open, and so perfectly still that the sound of all others most delicious to his ears—the gentle ripple of the Tweed over its pebbles—was distinctly audible as we knelt around the bed, and his eldest son kissed and closed his eyes. No sculptor ever marbled a more majestic image of repose."

He does not mention the taking of the death-mask, however, and nowhere alludes to it. It was made by George Bullock—it is said, at the request of Dr. Spurzheim—and Bullock and Chantrey both used it in modelling posthumous busts of the bard. It was loaned to Sir (then Mr.) Edwin Landseer while he was painting his full-length portrait of Sir Walter, with the background of the scenery of the Rhymer's Glen.

Bullock supposed that the original mould was destroyed not long after Scott's death, but Mr. Gourlay Steel writes that his brother, Sir John Steel, while engaged upon the monument to Lockhart at Dryburgh Abbey, some years later, came upon it accidentally at Abbotsford, and used it in remodelling his bust of Sir Walter for Mr. Hope-Scott.

Chantrey, in comparing the measurements of Scott's head from this mask with the measurements he had made of the head of Shakspere on the Stratford monument—which latter he had always considered unnatural, if not impossible—found, to his great surprise, that they were almost identical in height from the eyes up; and in each case he noticed the very unusual length of the upper-lip. It was this dome-like feature of Scott's head which inspired one of his jocular friends in Edinburgh to hail him once, when he dragged himself up the stairs of the Session House with his hat in his hand, as "Peveril of the Peak."

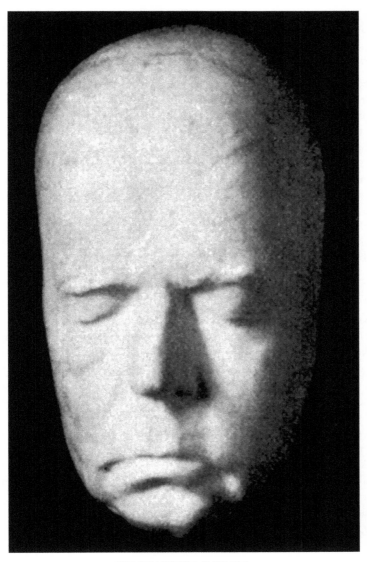

SIR WALTER SCOTT

When Carlyle last saw Scott—they never met to exchange a word—it was in one of the streets of Edinburgh, late in Scott's life; and, "Alas!" wrote the younger man, "his fine Scottish face, with its shaggy honesty and goodness, was all worn with care, the joy all fled from it, and ploughed deep with labor and sorrow."

Eighteen months after the death of Scott, the Burns mausoleum at Dumfries was opened to receive the remains of Burns's widow, when, according to the appendix to the first edition of Allan Cunningham's *Life of Burns*, then going through the press, a cast was taken from the cranium of the poet. Mr. Archibald Blacklock, surgeon of Dumfries, who made the examination, declared that "the cranial bones were perfect in every respect, and were firmly held together by their sutures," etc., etc. Unfortunately there is no cast of the head of the poet, living or dead, except this one here shown of his fleshless skull. George Combe, who received a replica of it from the executors of Mrs. Burns, presented a number of wood-cuts of it, in various positions, in his *Phrenology*, and he was very fond of using it to point his morals.

It is unusually large, even for the skull of a Scotchman; and viewed laterally, its length, due to the magnitude of the anterior lobe, is enormous.

Combe frequently reproduced the skull of Robert the Bruce, shown here as well, although he failed to explain the mystery of its existence in plaster. The skeletons of Bruce and his queen were discovered early in the present century by a party of workmen who were making certain repairs in the Abbey Church of Dunfermline. The bones of the hero of Bannockburn were identified from the description of the interment in contemporary records, and from the fact that the ribs on the left side had been roughly sawn away when the heart was delivered to Sir James Douglas, and sent off on its pious and romantic, but unsuccessful, pilgrimage to the Holy Land. The skull of Bruce, in an excellent state of preservation, was examined carefully by the Phrenological Society of Edinburgh, then in the highest tide of its enthusiasm and prosperity; and with the consent of the Crown, this cast of it was made. A gentleman who wrote anonymously to *Notes and Queries*, August 27, 1859, some forty years later, said that he remembered distinctly seeing and handling this skull, and the great sensation its discovery created. It was reinterred in its original resting-place a day or two later.

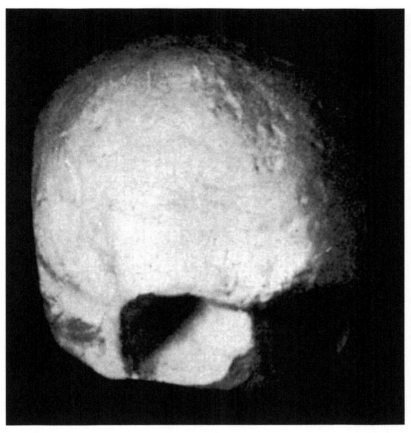

ROBERT BURNS

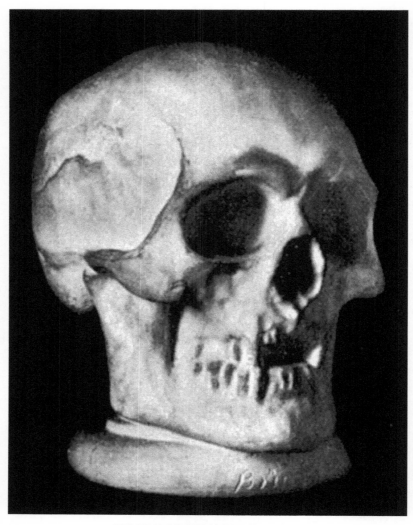

KING ROBERT THE BRUCE

The London *Times* contained, not very long ago, the following curious advertisement: "Napoleon I. For sale, the original mask moulded at Saint Helena by Dr. Antomarchi. Price required, £6000. Address," etc., etc.

Dr. F. Antomarchi, a native of Corsica, and a professor of anatomy at Florence, at the request of Cardinal Fesch and of "Madame Mère," and with the consent of the British government, went to Saint Helena in 1819 as physician to the exiled Emperor. He closed his master's eyes in death; and immediately before the official *post-mortem* examination, held the next day, he made the mask in question. He said in his report that the face was relaxed, but that the mask was correct so far as the shape of the forehead and nose was concerned. And unquestionably it is the most truthful portrait of Bonaparte that exists.

When Napoleon thought himself closely observed, he had, according to Sir Walter Scott, "the power of discharging from his countenance all expression save that of an indefinite smile, and presenting to the curious investigator the fixed and rigid eyes of a marble bust." As he is here observed, no matter how curiously or how closely, he is seen as he was. It is the face of Napoleon off his guard.

Bonaparte's distinguishing traits were selfishness, combativeness, destructiveness, acquisitiveness, secretiveness, self-esteem, and love of approbation. He had some vague notion of benevolence and of veneration, but he was blind to the dictates of truth and of justice, and he was so utterly deficient in conscientiousness that he does not seem to have been conscious of its existence.

His entire character was summed up once in four broken-English words, by an ignorant little local guide in Berlin. Fritz, showing a party of Americans through the royal palace at Charlottenburg, worked himself up to a pitch of patriotic frenzy in describing the conduct of the parvenu French Emperor during his occupancy of the private apartments of the legitimate German Queen, and he concluded his harangue by saying, quietly and decidedly, "But then, you know, Napoleon was no gentleman!"

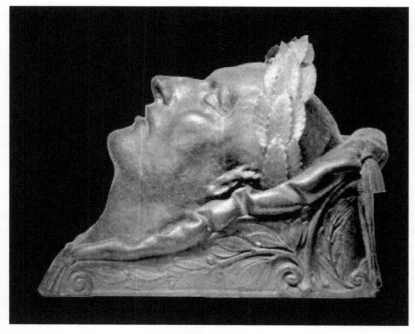

NAPOLEON I.

That seems to tell the whole story. He was, in his way, the greatest man who ever lived. He stepped from a humble cradle in an Italian provincial town on to the throne of France; he made his commonplace brothers and sisters and his ignorant henchmen kings and queens of all the European countries within his reach; he locked a pope in a closet, as if he had been a naughty boy; he re-drew the map of half the world; he re-wrote history; his name will live as long as books are read; no man out of so little ever accomplished so much—but yet he was *no* gentleman!

The Bonaparte mask, in bronze, as here shown is very rare. Only four are known to exist. The copy in the Paris Mint—*Hotel des Monnaies*—is without the gilded wreath which this copy possesses. It is said to have "been taken from the Emperor's face at St. Helena, twenty hours after his death."

The mask of Napoleon III. was taken, of course, at Chiselhurst. Louis Napoleon Bonaparte was distinguished, particularly, as being the only Bonaparte, for four generations at least, who bore no resemblance whatever to the Bonaparte family, not one of the strongly marked facial traits so universal in the tribe appearing in him.

No matter what may have been his shortcomings in other respects, he was devoted to his mother and to her memory. She used to call him "the mildly obstinate;" and the maternal judgment, perhaps, was mildly correct. Kinglake expressed it more epigrammatically when he said that "his characteristic was a faltering boldness." The historian of the Crimea, in his account of the attempt at Strasburg in 1836, pictured Prince Louis as "a young man with the bearing and the countenance of a weaver—a weaver oppressed by long hours of monotonous in-door work, which makes the body stoop and keeps the eyes downcast." Those half-shut eyes impressed every one who saw the Third Napoleon in life. He was called by Madden, in his *Memoirs of the Countess of Blessington*, "the man with the heavy eyelids, with the leaden hand of care and calculation pressing them down—the man-mystery, the depths of whose duplicity no Œdipus has yet sounded— the man with the pale, corpse-like, imperturbable features." Neither Mr. Kinglake nor the chosen biographer of the Blessingtons, however, was an impartial witness. Henry Wikoff, on the other hand, declared that his face recorded resolution, and that his eyes, which he kept half closed, revealed subtlety as well as daring. "His manner," according to the Chevalier, "was graceful, composed, and very *distingué*. He had the air of a man superior by nature as by birth." And Mrs. Browning believed in him and trusted him, and called him "the good and the just." He was perhaps the mildest-mannered man who ever scuttled ship of State, or cut a political throat.

NAPOLEON III.

The cast of the dead face of Oliver Cromwell, which was for some years in the cabinet of the Mint at Washington, bears the following inscription—copied *verbatim*:

> *This Mask is from the*
> *original one descended*
> *from Richard, Protector*
> *in poss: Mrs. Russell*
> *Chesthunt Park.*

BORN		DIED
1626	RICHARD	1712
	left them to his dau.	
1650	ELIZABETH	1731
	to her cousins	
1695	RICHARD—THOMAS	
1759	left the mask	
	to his dau:	
	ANNE ELIZ EX^ctrs.	
	they left it to	
	OLIVER CROMWELL	
	he left it to	
	his daughter	
	MRS. RUSSELL.	

In 1859 it was presented by Henry M. Field, Queen's Assay Master at the London Mint, and a direct descendant of Cromwell, to the late William E. Du Bois, who was for nearly half a century an officer of the mint at Washington. Shortly before his death the latter gentleman removed it to his own house; and it is now in the possession of his son, Mr. Patterson Du Bois of Philadelphia, through whose kindness the pedigree given is here printed.

Cromwell, according to the *Commonwealth Mercury* of November 23, 1658, was buried that day at the east end of the chapel of Henry VII., in Westminster Abbey. Dean Stanley accepted this as an established fact, notwithstanding the several reports, long current, that the body was thrown into the Thames, or laid in the field of Naseby, or carried to the vault of the Claypoles in the parish church of Northampton, or stolen during a heavy tempest in the night, or placed in the coffin of Charles I. at Windsor, Mr. Samuel Pepys being responsible for the last wild statement. After the Restoration this same Mr. Pepys saw the disinterred head of Cromwell in the *interior* of Westminster Hall, although all the other authorities agree in stating that, with the heads of Ireton and Bradshaw, it adorned the outer walls of that building.

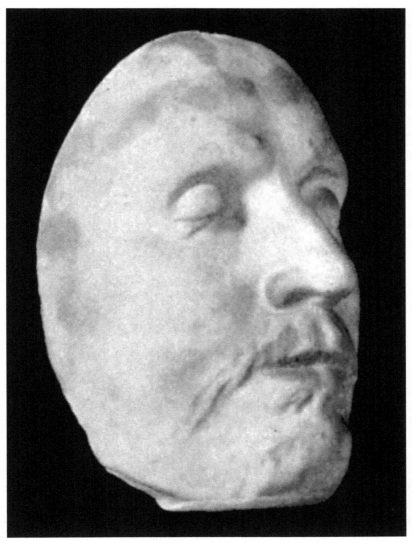

OLIVER CROMWELL

It may be stated, by the way, that a trustworthy friend of Mr. Pepys, and a fellow-diarist, one John Evelyn, witnessed "the superb funerall of the Lord Protector." He was carried from Somerset House in a velvet bed-of-state to Westminster Abbey, according to this latter authority; and "it was the joyfullest funerall I ever saw, for there were none that cried but dogs, which the soldiers hooted away with a barbarous noise, drinking and taking tobacco in the streets as they went." It does not seem to have occurred to Mr. Evelyn, or to other eye-witnesses of the funeral, that this was a mock ceremonial, and that the actual body of the Protector was not in the hearse.

Both Horace Smith and Cyrus Redding, early in the present century, saw what they fully believed to be the head of Cromwell. It was then in the possession of "a medical gentleman" in London. "The nostrils," said Redding, "were filled with a substance like cotton. The brain had been extracted by dividing the scalp. The membranes within were perfect, but dried up, and looked like parchment. The decapitation had evidently been performed after death, as the state of the flesh over the vertebræ of the neck plainly showed."

A correspondent of the London *Times*, signing himself "Senex," wrote to that journal, under date December 31, 1874, a full history of this head, in which he explained that at the end of five-and-twenty years it was blown down one stormy night, and picked up by a sentry, whose family sold it to one of the Cambridgeshire Russells, who were the nearest living descendants of the Cromwells. By them it was sold, and it was exhibited at several places in London. "Senex" gave the following account of the recognition of the head by Flaxman, the sculptor: "Well," said Flaxman, "I know a great deal about the configuration of the head of Oliver Cromwell. He had a low, broad forehead, large orbits to his eyes, a high septum to the nose, and high cheekbones; but there is one feature which will be with me a crucial test, and that is that instead of having the lower jawbone somewhat curved, it was particularly short and straight, but set out at an angle, which gave him a jowlish appearance. The head," continued "Senex," "exactly answered to the description, and Flaxman went away expressing himself as convinced and delighted." Another, and an earlier account, dated 1813, says that "the countenance has been compared by Mr. Flaxman, the statuary, with a plaster cast of Oliver's face taken after his death [of which there are several in London], and he [Flaxman] declares the features are perfectly similar."

Whether or not the body of the real Cromwell was dug up at the Restoration, and whether his own head, or that of some other unfortunate, was exposed on a spike to the fury of the elements for a quarter of a century on Westminster Hall, are questions which, perhaps, will never be decided. The head which Flaxman saw, as it is to be found engraved in contemporary prints, is not the head the cast of which is now in my possession, although it bears a certain resemblance thereto. Mine is probably "the cast from the face taken [immediately] after his death," of which, as we have seen, several copies were known to exist in Flaxman's time. It is, at all events, very like to the Cromwell who has been handed down to posterity by the limners and the statuaries of his own court. Thomas Carlyle was familiar with it, and believed in it, and he avowedly based upon it his famous picture of the Protector: "Big massive head, of somewhat leonine aspect; wart above the right eyebrow; nose of considerable blunt aquiline proportions; strict yet copious lips, full of all tremulous sensibility, and also, if need were, of all fierceness and rigor; deep, loving eyes, call them grave, call them stern, looking from under those shaggy brows as if in lifelong sorrow, and yet not thinking it sorrow, thinking it only labor and endeavor; on the whole, a right noble lion-face and hero-face; and to me it was royal enough."

The copy of the Cromwell mask in the Library of Harvard College is thus inscribed: "A cast from the original mask taken after death, once owned by Thomas Woolner, Sculptor. It was given by him to Thomas Carlyle, who gave it, in 1873, to Charles Eliot Norton, from whom Harvard College received it in 1881."

A copy of this mask in plaster is in the office of the National Portrait Gallery, in Great George Street, Westminster; and a wax mask, resembling it strongly, although not identical with it, is to be seen in the British Museum. This latter, which is broken in several places, lacks the familiar wart above the right eyebrow. There is no record of either of these casts in either institution, and the authorities and experts of both have no knowledge as to how and when they found their way to their present resting-places. Rev. Mark Noble, in his *House of Cromwell*, however, said that the representative in London of Ferdinand II., of Tuscany, bribed an attendant of Cromwell to permit him to take in secret "a mask of the Protector in plaster of Paris, which was done only a few moments after his Highness's dissolution." "A cast from this mould," he added, "is now in the Florentine Gallery. It is either of bronze, with a brassy hue, or stained to give it that appearance." Elsewhere Mr. Noble said, writing in 1737, that "the baronial family of Russell are in possession of a wax mask of Oliver, which is supposed to have been taken off while he was living."

After a careful study of all the Florentine galleries in the winter of 1892-93, I failed to find this copy of the Cromwell mask or any record of its ever having existed there, although the Pitti Palace contains an original portrait of Cromwell from life by Sir Peter Lely, which was presented by the Protector to this same Grand Duke Ferdinand II.

The mask of Henry IV., that darling king whose praises still the Frenchmen sing, has also a curious history. During the French Revolution, as is well known, the tombs of the Bourbons and the Valois at St. Denis were desecrated by the citizens of the republic. And when they began to "empty the rat-hole under the high altar," to use the words of one of their own leaders, the first coffin they came upon was that of Henry of Navarre. The body was discovered to have been carefully embalmed, and it was enveloped in a series of narrow bands of linen, steeped in some chemical preparation. The face was so well preserved that even the fan-shaped beard seemed as if it had been but recently dressed. The upper part of the brain had been removed, and was replaced by a sponge filled with aromatic essences. Enormous crowds came from Paris to look upon what was left of the monarch who once wished that all his subjects might have capon for their Sunday dinners; and undoubtedly some one of them made this cast of his face. It is still a common object in the plaster shops of Paris; and, painted a dark green to match the lintel of his door, it serves to-day as a sign and a symbol for a dealer in plaster images who does business in one of the side streets near upper Broadway, New York.

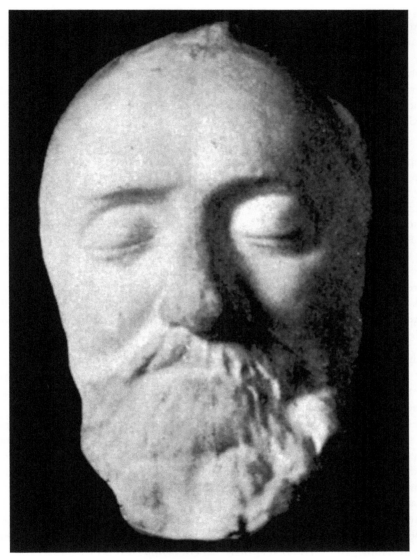

HENRY IV. OF FRANCE

M. Germain Bapst, writing in the *Gazette des Beaux Arts*, October, 1891, described a bust of Henry in wax which is preserved at Chantilly; and he proved it to be the work of G. Dupré, who, according to Malherbe, a contemporary historian, went to the Louvre the day after the king's death to make the wax effigy for his funeral, and took with him the modeller, who made a cast from the king's features. Concerning this cast itself the writer was silent; but he stated, although without giving his authority, that the plaster cast here reproduced dates back only to the time of the exhumation.

A scarce contemporary French engraving, entitled "Henri IV. Exhumé," represents the king as standing upright in an open coffin, against one of the great stone pillars in the vaults of St. Denis. The body is wrapped in strips of cloth, like an Egyptian mummy, but the head and shoulders are entirely exposed. A long inscription, at the bottom of the print, explains that "on this occasion a plaster cast was taken of the face—*on a moulé sur la nature même le plâtre*—from which to-day artists make their portraits of the great sovereign. The drawing upon which this engraving is based was executed by an eyewitness, and it shows the exact and marvellous state of preservation in which the body of the founder of the Bourbons was discovered. There was an effort made by the National Assembly to preserve this precious relic; but, alas, it was too late." The original mask of Henry is now in the Library of Ste. Geneviève, in Paris.

Charles XII. of Sweden was a soldier and little else. He knew no such word as fear. He was haughty and inflexible. He never thought of consulting the happiness of his people. He ascended the throne of a nation rich, powerful, and happy; he died king of a country which was ruined, wretched, and defenceless. Whether or not he was killed by one of his own soldiers, history has never been able to determine. He was shot in the head at the siege of Frederickshald, in Norway, in 1718; and when his body was exhumed and examined, a hundred and fifty years later, "the centre of his forehead was found to be disfigured by a depression corresponding with a fracture of that part of the skull." The fatal missile had passed entirely through the King's head from left to right in a downward direction; and in the cast in my collection the indentures, particularly the larger one on the right temple, are clearly perceptible. An engraving of this death-mask, dated 1823, contains the legend that it was "made four hours after he was shot, and was taken from the original cast preserved in the University Library at Cambridge, by Angelica Clarke."

CHARLES XII. OF SWEDEN

The copy of this cast in the British Museum is from the Christy collection. Henry Christy is known to have been in Stockholm at the time of the sale of the effects of Baestrom, the Swedish sculptor, and he is believed to have purchased it then and there. It contains more of the top and back of the head than the cast here reproduced, and it bears, very unmistakably, evidences of the bullet wounds in the temples. This cast, the wax mask of Cromwell mentioned above, and a cast of the face of James II. of England, are the only things of the kind the British Museum possesses.

Lavater wrote with unbounded enthusiasm of the impression made upon him by the face of Frederick the Great, whom he once saw in life. "Of all the physiognomies I have ever examined," he said, "there is not a single one which bears so strongly as this does the impress of its high destiny. The forehead, which forms almost a straight and continued line with the nose, announces impatience against the human race, and communicates the expression of it to the cheeks and lips," etc. And Mr. Fowler, who knew Frederick only by his portraits, ascribed to him fine temperament, intense mentality, great clearness and sharpness of thought, with a tendency to scholarship, and especially to languages, and with immense acquisitiveness.

Carlyle wrote: "All next day the body [of Frederick] lay in state in the Palace; thousands crowding, from Berlin and the other environs, to see the face for the last time. Wasted, worn, but beautiful in death, with the thin gray hair parted into locks and slightly powdered. And at eight in the evening, Friday, 18th [of August, 1786], he was borne to the Garrison-kirche of Potsdam, and laid beside his father in the vault behind the pulpit there."

The original of this cast of Frederick the Great is in the Hohenzollern Museum in Berlin, and of course is authentic. My own copy I brought from Berlin some ten years ago, with the consent of the authorities of the Museum.

FREDERICK THE GREAT

Concerning the personal appearance of General Grant, Mr. William A. Purrington, of New York, thus writes in a private letter, which he has kindly permitted me to make public:

"When I first knew the General I was a school-boy, and of course felt the school-boy's awe of a great man. Privileged to know him for years in the intimacy of his own home, I never entirely overcame that feeling. What was heroic in him grew, and did not diminish. The more I saw of him the more I felt that he was good as well as great. His face used to be called sphinx-like. That was scarcely true, for although its expression was always calm, strong, imperturbable, it was also one of great gentleness. He surely was a gentleman. Perhaps his hands aided to keep his face serene, for we must all have some safety-valve. Almost the only external indication of annoyance I ever noticed in him was a nervous opening and shutting of his fingers, an index of emotion often observed by other of his more intimate friends. A notable illustration of this trait was told me by a gentleman who once accompanied him to a large public dinner given in his honor. At its close one of the guests ventured upon the telling of stories which are not told *pueris virginibusque*. The General's fingers began to work; he quietly excused himself; and his companion, who knew the significance of the gesture, followed him. As they smoked their cigars on the streets of the foreign city in which this occurred, the General said: 'I hope I have not taken you from the table, but I have never permitted such conversation in my presence, and I never intend to.' This was not an affectation. His mind, clear and wholesome, left its imprint in his face. Grossness or scandal gave him genuine discomfort. He loved to think well of his kind. This trait showed in his face, gave it benignity, and was, I fancy, the secret of his hold on the affections of men. We chanced to be alone in his room one night after the last cruel betrayal of his confidence, he walking to and fro by the aid of his crutch. Suddenly he stopped, and, as if following aloud the train of his silent thought, he said: 'I have made it a rule of my life to believe in a man long after others have given him up. I do not see how I can do so again.' There was no bitterness in his voice, not even an elevation of tone. It was simply an exclamation of an honest heart sorely wounded in its belief.

"As I recall his face, that which I remember is not so much line and contour as the expression of strength, of great patience, of calmness, and of gentleness; and the incidents which illustrate pure qualities also come back freshly to my memory.

U. S. GRANT

"He had, too, a merry face; at times a merry eye. He was full of sly humor. The twinkling of his eye and his quiet laugh promptly rewarded an amusing story. In his own home his face was always kind and responsive. There he was not the silent man the world thought it knew, but a fluent and well-informed talker on all that was of interest to him. Undoubtedly, however, he had the gift of silence, and when he saw fit to exercise it his face became a mask, conversation ceased to be among the possibilities, and a chat with a graven image would have been a relief at such a time. He became then, and designedly, a silence-compeller. When there was nothing to be said, he said nothing."

General Grant, on the occasion of the surrender of General Lee at Appomattox Court House, was thus described by General Horace Porter, his aide-de-camp: "He was then nearly forty-three years of age, five feet eight inches in height, with shoulders slightly stooped. His hair and full beard were a nut-brown, without a trace of gray. He had on a single-breasted blouse, made of dark-blue flannel, unbuttoned in front, and showing a waistcoat underneath. He wore an ordinary pair of top-boots, with his trousers inside and without spurs. The boots and portions of his clothes were spattered with mud. He had had on a pair of thread gloves of a dark yellow color, which he had taken off on entering the room. His felt 'sugar-loaf,' stiff-brimmed hat was thrown on the table beside him. He had no sword, and a pair of shoulder straps was all there was about him to designate his rank. In fact, aside from these, his uniform was that of a private soldier."

This was thoroughly characteristic of the simplicity and modesty of the man. He came, in the face of the whole admiring world, to make his lasting mark upon one of the most important pages of his country's history, the General of his country's armies, perhaps the greatest soldier of his time, without a spur and without a sword, in the well-worn uniform of a private of Volunteers.

He died as bravely and as quietly as he had lived, like one who had even studied in his death to throw away the dearest thing he owned, as 'twere a careless trifle. He sleeps now on the banks of the Hudson, in that enduring, honorable peace for which he had fought so long, and which he had won so gloriously. His body was greatly wasted by lingering disease, but those who saw him immediately after death say that his face looked ten years younger than it had looked during the previous trying months.

The cast of Grant here presented is still in the possession of his family in New York; and it is the only copy ever made with their consent, and to their knowledge.

WILLIAM T. SHERMAN

Of General Sherman, General Porter said: "He was a many-sided man, who had run the entire gamut of human experience. He had been merchant, banker, lawyer, professor, traveller, author, doctor, president of a street railway, and soldier. Wherever he was placed, his individuality was conspicuous and pronounced. His methods were always original, and even when unsuccessful they were entertaining. He could not have been commonplace if he had tried." There was certainly nothing commonplace in his personal appearance. His frame was tall and wiry; his hazel eyes were sharp and penetrating; his nose was aquiline; his beard was short and crisp; his mouth was firm and tender; his bearing was courtly, unpretentious, and dignified. He was the typical soldier in appearance and action; like Grant, he was entirely devoid of any outward expression of vanity, self-esteem, or self-consciousness. As he was one of the bravest, so was he one of the gentlest, kindest, most sympathetic of men. The mask of General Sherman was made immediately after his death, under the direction of Mr. St. Gaudens.

Washington was as blessed in his death as in his life. He rests still upon the banks of the Potomac, among the people whom he so dearly loved and among whom he died; and no later administration has ever cared to cut off his head for exhibition on the roof of the Patent Office or the Smithsonian Institution.

At least two plaster casts were taken from the living face of Washington. The first, by Joseph Wright, in 1783, was broken by the nervous artist before it was dry; and the subject absolutely, and, it is whispered, profanely, refused to submit to the unpleasant operation again. The second was made by Houdon, the celebrated French sculptor, in 1785, and from it was modelled the familiar bust which bears Houdon's name.

The original Houdon mask of Washington is now in the possession of Mr. W. W. Story, in his studio in Rome. He traces it directly from Houdon's hands, and naturally he prizes it very highly. It has been preserved with great care, and of it he says "there is no question that it was made from the living face of Washington, and that therefore it is the most absolutely authentic representation of the actual forms and features of his face that exists. In all respects, any portrait which materially differs from it must be wrong." Mr. Story cannot account for the fact that the sculptor opened the eyes of Washington in the mask, except upon the supposition that he did not remain long enough at Mount Vernon to have studied and modelled the eyes for his bust from the face of Washington himself.

GEORGE WASHINGTON

It is but just to add here that Mr. Story says that never, to his knowledge or belief, has a cast been made from the original which he owns. He examined the so-called cast in the Corcoran Gallery at Washington, and he was fully satisfied that, like all the other specimens in existence, it is of no value in itself, and was made from a worn-out copy of the bust. The Washington mask here presented is from a photograph taken by Mr. Story in Rome, and from his own copy.

The attempt of the sculptor Browere to take a life-mask of Thomas Jefferson was not more successful, and was much more disastrous, than Wright's attempt upon the face of Washington. Mr. Ben Perley Poore quotes Clark Mills as telling the following story: "The family of the ex-President were opposed to it, but he finally consented, saying that he could not find it in his heart to refuse a man so trifling a favor who had come so far. He was placed on his back on a sofa, one of his hands grasping a chair which stood in front. Not dreaming of any danger, his family could not bear to see him with the plaster over his face, and therefore were not present; and his faithful Burwell was the only person besides the artist in the room. There was some defect in the arrangements made to permit his breathing, and Mr. Jefferson came near suffocating. He was too weak to rise or to relieve himself, and his feeble struggles were unnoticed or unheeded by his Parrhasius.

"The sufferer finally bethought himself of the chair on which his hand rested. He raised it as far as he was able, and struck it on the floor. Burwell became conscious of his situation, and sprang furiously forward. The artist shattered his cast in an instant. The family now reached the room, and Browere looked as if he thought their arrival most opportune, for though Burwell was supporting his master in his arms, the fierce glare of the African eye boded danger. Browere was permitted to pick up his fragments of plaster and carry them off, but whether he ever put them together to represent features emaciated with age and debility, and writhing in suffocation, Mills did not know."

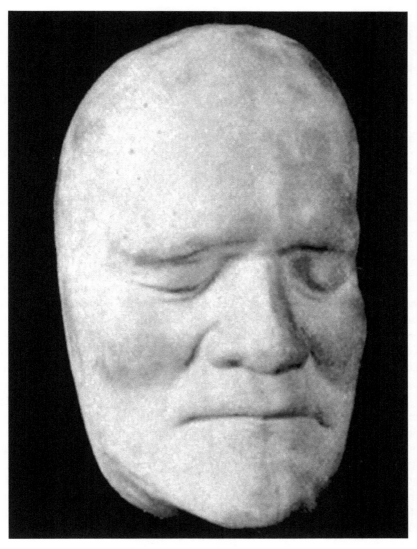

BENJAMIN FRANKLIN

The mask of Jefferson in the fragmentary condition described above would be of little value even if it had been preserved.

When Houdon came to America in 1785 to make the bust of Washington, he was the companion of Benjamin Franklin, and he was, in all probability, the author of this cast of Franklin's face, taken in Paris that year as a model for the well-known Houdon bust of Franklin, which it somewhat resembles. The original mask was sold in Paris for ten francs after the death of the artist in 1828.

The familiars of Franklin have shown that his face in his old age changed in a very marked degree. He was in his seventy-eighth or his seventy-ninth year when he sat for Houdon in 1784-85. Many of the features of the Franklin cast as here reproduced—the long square chin, the sinking just beneath the under lip, the shape of the nose, and the formation of the cheekbones—are strongly preserved in the face of one of his great-granddaughters now living in Philadelphia.

Leigh Hunt in his *Autobiography* said that Franklin and Thomas Paine were frequently guests at the house of his maternal grandfather in Philadelphia when his mother was a girl. She remembered them both distinctly; and in her old age she told her son that while she had great affection and admiration for Franklin, Paine "had a countenance that inspired her with terror." Hunt was inclined to attribute this in a great measure to Paine's political and religious views, both of them naturally obnoxious and shocking to the daughter of a Pennsylvania Tory and rigid churchman. Concerning the physical as well as the moral traits of the author of the *Age of Reason*, there seems to have been great diversity of opinion. To paraphrase the speech of Griffith in *Henry VIII.* concerning Wolsey, He was uncleanly and sour to them that loved him not, but to those men that sought him, sweet and fragrant as summer. His friend and biographer, Clio Rickman, who considered him "a very superior character to Washington," gave strong testimony to his personal attractions and tidiness of dress; while James Cheetham, his biographer and not his friend, told a very different and not a very pleasant story, in which soap and water—or their absence—play an important part. The former, according to Cheetham, was never employed externally by Paine, and the latter was very rarely, if ever, internally applied.

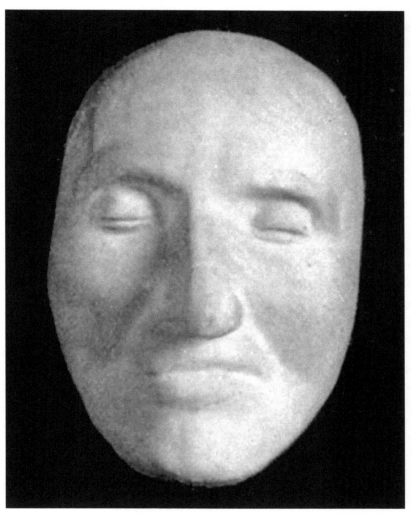

THOMAS PAINE

None of his earlier biographers give any hint as to the taking of this death-mask, nor is it to be found in any contemporary printed account of the death-bed scene, although Mr. Moncure D. Conway, in his *Life of Paine*, published in 1892, accepts it as genuine, and ascribes it to Jarvis. All the experts agree that it is the face of Paine, and see in it a strong resemblance to the face in the Romney portrait, painted in 1792, seventeen years before Paine died. It was undoubtedly made after death, by John Wesley Jarvis, the painter, who was at one time an intimate of Paine. He studied modelling in clay, and made the bust of Paine which is now in the possession of the Historical Society of New York. Concerning this bust Dr. Francis, in his *Old New York*, wrote: "The plaster cast of the head and features of Paine, now preserved in the Gallery of Arts of the Historical Society, is remarkable for its fidelity to the original at the close of his life. Jarvis, the painter, then felt it his most successful work in that line of occupation, and I can confirm the opinion from my many opportunities of seeing Paine." He added that Jarvis said, "I shall secure him to a nicety if I am so fortunate as to get plaster enough for his carbuncled nose," which was not a very pretty speech to have made under any circumstances, particularly if the bust was executed after the subject's death.

The death-mask of Aaron Burr was made by an agent of Messrs. Fowler & Wells, who still possess the original cast. The features are shortened in a marked degree by the absence of the teeth. Mr. Fowler said that "in Burr destructiveness, combativeness, firmness, and self-esteem were large, and amativeness excessive." It is a curious fact, now generally forgotten, that Burr and Hamilton resembled each other in face and figure in a very marked degree, although Burr was a trifle the taller.

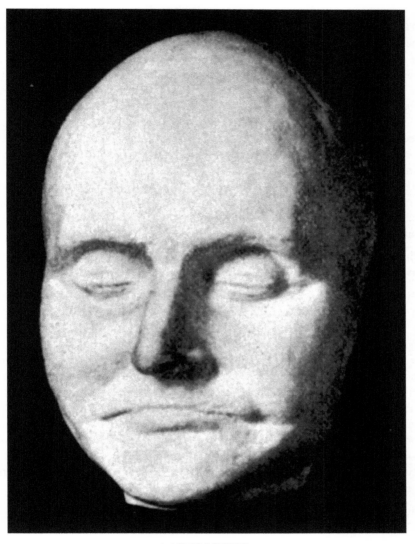

AARON BURR

A bust of Burr by Turnerelli, an Italian sculptor residing in London during the first decade of the century, was exhibited at the Royal Academy in 1809; and Burr, in his *Diary and Letters*, spoke more than once of the cast of his face made by the sculptor at that time. He explained to Theodosia that he "submitted to the very unpleasant ceremony because Turnerelli said it was necessary," and because Bentham and others had undergone a similar penance; and in his *Diary* he wrote: "Casting my eyes in the mirror, I observed a great purple mark on my nose; went up and washed and rubbed it, all to no purpose. It was indelible. That cursed mask business has occasioned it. I believe the fellow used quicklime instead of plaster of Paris, for I felt a very unpleasant degree of heat during the operation.... I have been applying a dozen different applications to the nose, which have only inflamed it. How many curses have I heaped upon that Italian!... At eleven went to Turnerelli to sit. Relieved myself by abusing him for that nose disaster.... He will make a most hideous frightful thing [of the bust]; but much like the original."

This mask, if it is still in existence—which is not probable—would be an invaluable addition to the portraiture of Burr.

Of Lincoln, as of Washington, two life-masks were made—one in Chicago in the spring of 1860, by Mr. Leonard W. Volk, and here reproduced; one in Washington, by Clark Mills, three or four years later. Mr. Volk, in the *Century Magazine* for December, 1881, gave a pleasant account of the taking of the former. Lincoln sat naturally in the chair during the operation, watching in a mirror every move made by the sculptor, as the plaster was put on without interference with the eyesight or with the breathing of the subject. When, at the end of an hour, the mould was ready for removal—it was in one piece, and contained both ears—Lincoln himself bent his head forward and worked it off gradually and gently, without injury of any kind, notwithstanding the fact that it clung to the high cheek-bones, and that a few hairs on his eyebrows and temples were pulled out by the roots with the plaster.

This is, without question, the most perfect representation of Lincoln's face in existence. I have watched many an eye fill while looking at it for the first time; to many minds it has been a revelation; and I turn to it myself more quickly and more often than to any of the others, when I want comfort and help. What Whittier wrote to James T. Fields of the Marshall engraving of Lincoln may be said of this life-cast. "It contains the informing spirit of the man within.... The old harsh lines and unmistakable mouth are there without flattery or compromise; but over all, and through all, the pathetic sadness, the wise simplicity, and tender humanity of the man are visible. It is the face of the speaker at Gettysburg, and the writer of the second Inaugural."

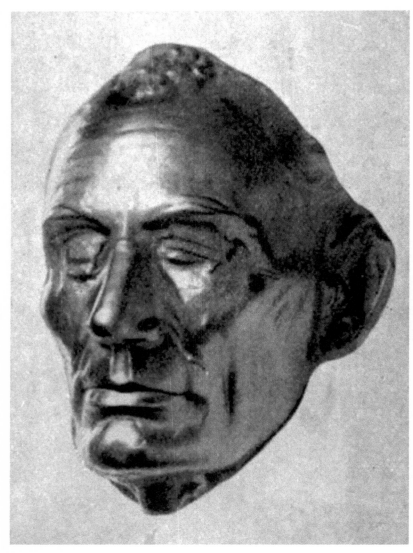

ABRAHAM LINCOLN

The Clark Mills mask, said Mr. John Hay, in a later number of the *Century Magazine*, is "so sad and peaceful in its infinite repose that the famous sculptor, Mr. St. Gaudens, insisted when he first saw it that it was a death-mask. The lines are set, as if the living face, like the copy, had been in bronze; the nose is thin, and lengthened by the emaciation of the cheeks; the mouth is fixed like that of an archaic statue; a look as of one on whom sorrow and care had done their worst, without hope of victory, is on all the features; the whole expression is of unspeakable sadness and all-sufficing strength. Yet the peace is not the dreadful peace of death; it is the peace that passeth understanding."

Speaking of Webster, Mr. O. F. Fowler, in his *Practical Phrenology*, said: "A larger mass of brain, perhaps, never was found, and never will be found, in the upper and lateral portions of any man's forehead. Both in height and in breadth his forehead is prodigiously great." The head of Clay, according to the same authority, was also "unusually large. It measured seven and three-eighths inches in diameter, and it was very high in proportion to its breadth; the reasoning organs were large, and the perceptive and semi-perceptive organs still larger." Mr. G. P. A. Healy, the painter, said that Mr. Clay's mouth was very peculiar; that it was thin-lipped, and extended from ear to ear. This last is not particularly noticeable in the familiar portraits of Clay, not even in that painted by Mr. Healy himself. Both Mr. St. Gaudens and Mr. Hartley incline to the opinion that the mask of Clay in my collection is a cast from the actual face, and, notwithstanding the fact that the eyelids are open, that it is from life. Lewis Gaylord Clark, writing in 1852 in HARPER'S MAGAZINE of Clay's funeral, said: "His countenance immediately after death looked like an antique cast. His features seemed to be perfectly classical, and the repose of all his muscles gave the lifeless body a quiet majesty seldom reached by living human beings."

Comparing Calhoun with Webster, Mr. Fowler attributed to Calhoun the greater power of analysis and illustration; to Webster, the greater depth and profundity. In Calhoun he found, united to a very large head, an active temperament and sharp organs, the greatest peculiarity of his phrenology consisting in the fact that *all* the intellectual faculties were very large. The casts of Webster and Calhoun were made in Washington by Clark Mills from the living faces—Calhoun's in 1844, Webster's in 1849; and they are, consequently, of no little interest and value.

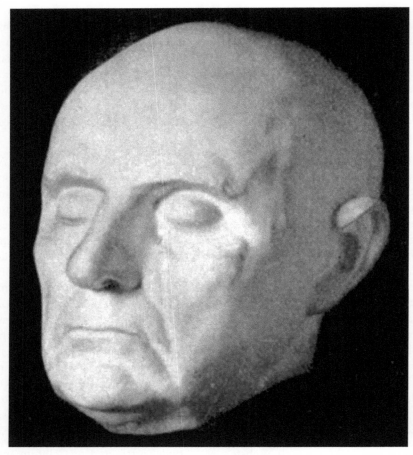

DANIEL WEBSTER

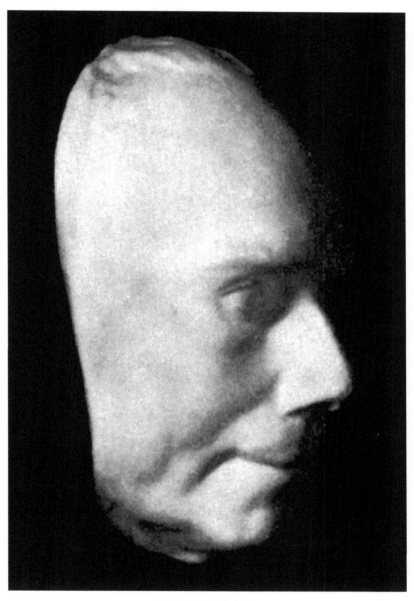

HENRY CLAY

JOHN C. CALHOUN

Sydney Smith, who once called Daniel Webster "a steam-engine in trousers," thus disposed of a contemporary British statesman: "Lord Brougham's great passions," he said, "are vanity and ambition. He considers himself as one of the most wonderful works of Providence, is incessantly striving to display that superiority to his fellow-creatures, and to grasp a supreme dominion over all men and all things. His vanity is so preposterous that it has exposed him to ludicrous failures, and little that he has written will survive him. His ambition, and the falsehood and intrigue with which it works, have estranged all parties from him, and left him, in the midst of bodily and intellectual strength, an isolated individual, whom nobody will trust, and with whom nobody will act."

The head of Brougham was of full size, but not unusual. A student of physiognomy, but not a student of the back numbers of the London *Punch*, who did not recognize the man in this cast, said of it that it was the head of a man more remarkable for vivacity and quickness of mind than for original and powerful thinking. George Combe, in the winter of 1838-39, exhibited in the United States a mask of Brougham, of course from life, for Brougham did not die until thirty years after that—and he was born in 1778—which is perhaps the mask here reproduced, as it is the face of a man in his prime, and his was a marvellous prime—not that of a nonogenarian. Brougham's powers of activity and endurance were phenomenal. It is recorded of him that he went from the Law Courts to the House of Commons, from the House to his own chambers, where he wrote an article for the *Edinburgh Review*, then, without rest, to the Courts and the House again, sitting until the morning of the third day before he thought of his bed or his sleep; and that during all this time he showed no signs of mental or physical fatigue. Such continuous activity certainly did not shorten his days, even if it lengthened his nights.

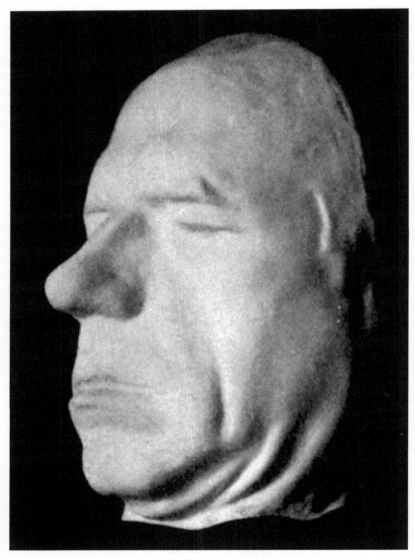

LORD BROUGHAM

Probably no single facial organ in the world has been the subject of so much attention from the caricaturists as the nose of Lord Brougham. It is doubtful if any two consecutive numbers of any so-called comic or satirical journal appeared in England during Brougham's time without some representation of Brougham's nose. The author of *Notes on Noses* thus spoke of it: "It is a most eccentric nose; it comes within no possible category; it is like no other man's; it has good points and bad points and no point at all. When you think it is going right on for a Roman, it suddenly becomes a Greek; when you have written it down cogitative, it becomes as sharp as a knife.... It is a regular Proteus; when you have caught it in one shape it instantly becomes another. Turn it and twist it and view it how, when, and where you will, it is never to be seen twice in the same shape; and all you can say of it is that it's a queer one. And such exactly," he added, "is my Lord Brougham.... Verily my Lord Brougham and my Lord Brougham's nose have not their likeness in heaven or earth.... And the button at the end is the cause of it all."

An interesting tribute to this remarkable organ is to be found in the printed *Correspondence of John Lothrop Motley*. Concerning Commemoration Day at Oxford he wrote, in 1860, "Nothing could be more absurd than Lord Brougham's figure, long and gaunt, with snow-white hair under the great black porringer, and his wonderful nose wagging lithely from side to side as he hitched up his red petticoats [Commemoration robes] and stalked through the mud."

There is no button on the end of the nose of the specimen of humanity whose mask forms a tail-piece to this volume. Cowper, Combe, and others believed that the brain of the native African is inferior in its intellectual powers to the brain of the man of European birth and descent, while a certain body of naturalists contend that the negro owes his present inferiority entirely to bad treatment and to unfavorable circumstances. The black boy, the cast of whose face was made for this collection at St. Augustine, Florida, by Mr. Thomas Hastings, the architect, a year or two ago, has undoubtedly been for generations the victim of unfavorable circumstances, and perhaps of bad treatment as well. He is, at all events, one of the lowest examples of his race, and his life-mask is only interesting here as an object of comparison. Whatever the head of a Bonaparte, a Washington, a Webster, or a Brougham is, his head is not. But whether his Creator or the Caucasian is responsible for this, the naturalists and experts must decide.

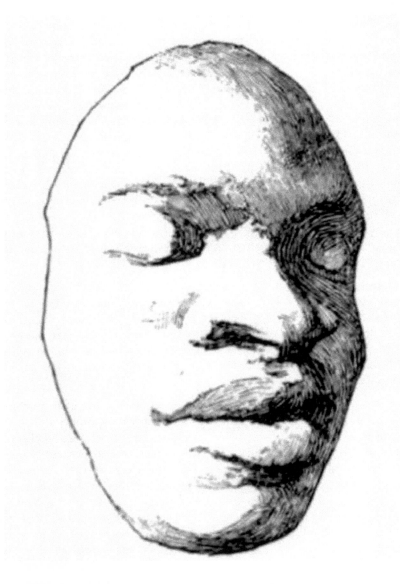

FLORIDA NEGRO BOY

Milton Keynes UK
Ingram Content Group UK Ltd.
UKHW021557260524
443160UK00005B/352